T0365109

LOVE *on* THE
Kitchen Table

A Couples' Guide to Creative
Communications and Lasting Love

ALEISHA COOTE

BALBOA.
PRESS

A DIVISION OF HAY HOUSE

Cover design by Chance Lockwood-Mawson. Front cover photograph from © iStockphoto.com, photograph by Andreas Reh Photography.

Interior image designs by Lydia Leong at GurlRilla Shots Photography.

Balboa Press books may be ordered through booksellers or by contacting:

Balboa Press
A Division of Hay House
1663 Liberty Drive
Bloomington, IN 47403
www.balboapress.com
1 (877) 407-4847

Because of the dynamic nature of the Internet, any web addresses or links contained in this book may have changed since publication and may no longer be valid. The views expressed in this work are solely those of the author and do not necessarily reflect the views of the publisher, and the publisher hereby disclaims any responsibility for them.

The author of this book does not dispense medical advice or prescribe the use of any technique as a form of treatment for physical, emotional, or medical problems without the advice of a physician, either directly or indirectly. The intent of the author is only to offer information of a general nature to help you in your quest for emotional and spiritual well-being. In the event you use any of the information in this book for yourself, which is your constitutional right, the author and the publisher assume no responsibility for your actions.

Any people depicted in stock imagery provided by Thinkstock are models, and such images are being used for illustrative purposes only.
Certain stock imagery © Thinkstock.

Printed in the United States of America.

ISBN: 978-1-4525-1198-6 (sc)
ISBN: 978-1-4525-1199-3 (e)

Balboa Press rev. date: 04/23/2014

Contents

Acknowledgements

Forever Grateful

Firstly I am forever grateful to the womb from which I came as the sacred place of creation and growth. I am grateful for the love and care I received within my core family network because this support assisted me to grow and seek the knowledge to serve others. To my extended family, thank you for sharing your world.

Secondly a message of continued love and appreciation goes to my dear husband. I have been raw, real, and ready to love you since the moment we met. Thank you for being so amazing. I could pray for nothing more in a man. Thank you for your love, commitment, acceptance, and protection. I am a better person for sharing my life with you.

Next a heartfelt thank-you goes to all the inspirational friends in my life. You know who you are. Together with the brilliant clients whom I have had the privilege of coaching over the years, I want to let you know you are all wonderful and inspiring. In serving you I have been served a million times over. By sharing in your adventures and journeys, I have been exposed to such varied reference points for the core needs of love, success, and happiness. You have opened your hearts to me and allowed a level of connection that is only possible through a filter of deep love and appreciation. A radiance exists within all of you, and the combination of this radiance has helped to make this book what it is.

To my mentors, coaches, and teachers, thank you. Thank you for living and breathing a commitment to the success of your students and for making ripples of change far beyond the boundaries of our knowledge.

To my favourite inspirational writers who have shared their words through my eyes, thank you. To all the shoulders of giants who have gone before me and allowed a platform from which to further develop my work, thank you.

This book is a reflection of the greatness I have encountered over the years. Author James Redfield once wrote, "The universe is energy, energy that responds to our expectations. People are part of that energy universe too, so when we have a question, the people show up who have the answer."

I have great expectations. Thank you to all of those who showed up to bring this book to fruition.

Forever grateful,
Aleisha Coote

Introduction

I was once told a horrific story about a jelly bean jar. After I proudly announced to a colleague that I was now engaged to marry the man of my dreams, his worried response asked if I was aware of the jelly bean philosophy? My brief philosophical encounter with Plato and Aristotle in high school classical studies had not covered this point, and given jelly beans didn't exist in Plato's days, I thought the modern theme of this guy's theory might be worth knowing. Curious, I enquired.

His philosophical metaphor stated the following: "When you meet someone and fall in love, you should purchase an empty jar."

His know-it-all expression scanned my reaction to make sure I was following. It sounded simple. I nodded.

He continued, "Every time you and your partner make love you should then add a single jelly bean to the jar."

I nodded to confirm my understanding once more.

"When you get married, you then place the lid on the jar."

Simple again.

"After your wedding day and honeymoon, you remove the lid of the jar, and every time you make love following your wedding date you remove one single jelly bean from the jar."

I waited in anticipation.

"You'll never empty it," he said, backed by a poor-you look on his face.

Ouch.

Rather than a kind congratulations towards my recent engagement, "Say goodbye to sex" was this guy's obvious theme.

"He is seriously screwed," said the response in my head.

However, "hmmm, interesting," were the words I heard come from my mouth.

Another unmarried expert once questioned me about a travel adventure I was researching. The location was a university cafeteria. I was flicking through a travel brochure, as my husband-to-be and I were planning a Contiki adventure across Europe.

Contiki tours can be commonly defined as party-focused travel adventures, specifically for eighteen- to thirty-five-year-olds.

The unmarried expert began his insight.

"Are you planning a Contiki trip?" he asked.

I recognised his face from one of my lectures. My interpersonal communications class came to mind, and I remembered that he sat in the back row. I nodded and began to explain our exciting plans to adventure through Europe on a Contiki tour later in the year. He told me of his own Contiki adventures from a few years ago and shared his highlights.

He then paused.

"Aren't you getting married?" he enquired.

"Yes," I stated proudly, wondering how he knew. Perhaps he had noticed my engagement ring.

"Well," he shared, "don't you know that married couples don't do Contiki?"

I was shocked. I'd read the brochure in full, yet nowhere in the fine print had I come across a clause that stated married couples weren't welcome.

"Tell me more," I enquired. At this point I wasn't sure if I liked this guy anymore.

And so he continued. "Married couples don't do Contiki because the tours are all about sex, drugs, and alcohol."

Interesting, I thought. *Does this guy seriously think that married couples don't have sex, don't know how to light a joint, and can't drink?*

"This guy is seriously screwed," said the response in my head.

But, "hmmm, interesting," were the words I heard come from my mouth.

And the experts continued to emerge from the woodwork. I've heard it all.

"You know it's all downhill from here," they said.

"Why would you get married so young? You have the rest of your life to live."

"Don't waste your life. You only live once."

Shocked and confused, as a by-product of our engagement I became quickly exposed to the limiting beliefs about marriage that existed within society. Following my subdued responses, I would go home and speak to my husband-to-be.

Okay, time for introductions. Tall, dark, and handsome, think along the lines of Eric from *The Little Mermaid*—and his name is Hayden. This book is based on our story, so he'll feature often, and I can fill you in as we go.

I would go home and speak with Hayden about the comments I had faced during the day. His standard response generally included, "Don't worry. All that really matters is how we feel." He might say, "Ignore them. We'll find a way to make our marriage work and prove them all wrong."

For the rational male mind, these quick-fix responses might serve a Band-Aid purpose, yet my ever-wondering female mind was far from satisfied. I recognised that these were the beliefs of others, not mine. Yet I also realised that on some level they were challenging my own beliefs, which were obviously not as sound as I may have first thought.

I've since learnt that a women's sense of self is defined through her feelings and the quality of her relationships. Looking back with this in mind, it makes sense that the combination of these moments brought me to the point where I realised I had two choices. I could continue to become consumed with the limiting beliefs of society and as a result send my own love life to meet a gradual, depressing, status-quo divorce, or I could go against the grain and get incredibly curious about what it took to do the exact opposite and instead create a successful and loving relationship. While the latter felt like it might take some hard work, the result of growing old with the one I loved and experiencing a lifetime of intimacy and fulfillment was far too attractive to turn down. I felt I was up for the challenge—and so the seed was planted.

I became fascinated in human behaviour and all things related to building a successful relationship. Together, Hayden and I set out to discover the fundamental elements of an intimate connection that transcended the limiting beliefs of society. We got curious. We asked questions. Most importantly we backed ourselves. As part of our journey I added a diploma in coaching and training to my degree in communications and public relations. Today I live and breathe all topics surrounding human behaviour, human consciousness, and human awareness. Together, Hayden and I have also completed our master practitioner training in neuro linguistic programming (NLP), studied the exploration of masculine and feminine energy, and trained in relationship and sex coaching. The adventure has taken us places far beyond our wildest dreams, and the results have had a profound impact on each of our lives, first at an individual level and then organically impacting the strength of our relationship. As a result of this profound impact, I have become completely committed to sharing what we've learnt with others. In 2010 I launched a coaching and training practice that focuses on personal coaching, professional development, and strengths-based strategies to generate results for people in life and business. Since this time I have had the pleasure of working with incredible clients around the globe, and throughout the years many of our conversations have centred on the theme of relationships. The fact that this topic comes up so regularly in both the personal and professional coaching work I do is because man was not created to exist in isolation, and the success (or lack of success) in our most intimate relationships has a direct impact on our overall happiness and fulfillment in life. While I explored this fundamental relationship theme over the years, I have come to find nine specific patterns that are most commonly addressed in the coaching work I do. It is these patterns that form the chapters of this book, and the themes make up the *Love on the Kitchen Table* model.

I am convinced the secret to a successful relationship is ultimately about creating your *own* blueprint for success. It's about getting connected with what is true for you and with the results you are committed to creating in your own life because we all have a choice. And if you are willing to acknowledge that choice and take 100 per cent responsibility for the results you are getting in your life right now, then you are ready to read on. A life less ordinary comes to those who are ready to step up and back themselves.

As you read this book, I challenge you to get clear on what it is you are truly committed to achieving in your relationship both with yourself and then with your significant other because the real journey begins from within. You must be willing to look within and work on your relationship with yourself in order to then connect on a new level with your loved one. Only when you are whole and true within can you then take the best version of yourself into your relationship and everyday world. Only when you are whole and true within can you then inspire others through a ripple effect of leadership in the space of love and connection. My model for delivery—an artistic metaphor and powerful symbol— is *Love on the Kitchen Table*.

I believe that the kitchen table has sadly become vacant in the modern family home. In fact, many homes these days don't even allow for kitchen table space. Population growth has led to a decrease in floor-plan sizes, and the dining room is often the first space to be strategically molded into an open-plan living area, a kitchen island, or a bar-top peninsula with stools. Yet in our quest to make way for additional storage, perceived space, and showcase designs, I believe what we have really sacrificed is the heart of the family home.

The kitchen table is a no-frills, practical, and serviceable piece of furniture. Despite its humble structure, the magic of the table can be found through its utilitarian role and lineage link—both of which fuel nostalgia and a strong tie to something so much more than four legs and a tabletop. The kitchen table is the place where kids sit to do their homework. It's where families enjoy their daily meals, where face-to-face interactions are fostered. It's tea and cookies, candles and a rose. It's clean. It's chipped. Chairs in. Chairs out. It's where you cut the birthday cake and divide the family roast. Pass the potatoes please. It's memories. It's relationships.

I am officially supporting a kitchen table revival and have chosen the metaphor of the table as the structure for this book. The kitchen table serves as a symbol for the foundations to building a successful relationship because the two have more similarities than may appear at first glance. While the kitchen table is a tangible item, relationships are mysterious and open to interpretation. Yet both are humble and often lost in our busy lives.

Throughout this book I will use the symbol of the kitchen table to share powerful insights on the fundamental elements that make up a successful relationship. Each chapter will work to explain one of the steps that make up the *Love on the Kitchen Table* nine-step metaphor for relationship success. In exploring each of the nine steps, you'll discover an array of insights that shine light on a process for reviving or enhancing your most intimate relationship. For those of you committed to true growth and success in this area, here's a brief snapshot of what lies ahead.

Chapter 1—Building the Table: Beliefs as the Foundation of a Relationship

In chapter 1 you'll set the scene with a reflection on a table's structure. Just as the legs of a table support the tabletop, your reference points for your beliefs in life support the structure of your relationships. For example, what are your beliefs about marriage? What are your beliefs about what it means to be a man? What are your beliefs about what it means to be a woman? This chapter will explore how your answers to these types of questions shape the foundations of your relationship. Weak foundations mean structural faults, and therefore your beliefs about love and marriage must be strong in order to support a solid tabletop.

Chapter 2—Lighting the Candles of Value: Understanding How Values Guide Relationships

In chapter 2 you'll explore the candles on the kitchen table as representations of the values that exist within your relationship. You'll discover the top five values that drive your decision-making processes and discover how every decision you make in life is based on your hierarchy of values. This chapter will teach you how to elicit and leverage your values to take control of the way you live your life. As part of this exploration, you will learn what drives your partner's thinking. Finally you will combine your insights to explore the unique combination that sets the atmosphere for your relationship.

Chapter 3—The Essential Tools: The Ten Core Needs of an Ideal Relationship

Chapter 3 introduces the relationship plate of core needs, highlighting the ten essential elements that make up a successful relationship, including an exploration of both individual needs and the needs of a relationship. Knowledge is power, and when you are clear on where to direct your focus, creating an ideal relationship then becomes easily attainable. This chapter provides the checklist for ensuring relationship success.

Chapter 4—The Special Touch on Setting the Table: Exploring Feminine Energy

Once the structure of the table is achieved, the candles of value are lit, and the essential tools are available to enjoy the meal, it is time to prepare and serve the food. Feminine energy ensures the table is arranged with love and that the kitchen and serving of the meal has an effortless flow. Chapter 4 will introduce the theory of masculine and feminine energy through reflection of yin and yang, central to Taoism, the universal principle that underlies all of creation. The yin-and-yang theory states that the world is made up of two opposing energies, yin (feminine) and yang (masculine). This chapter will explore the re-emergence of the feminine power and demonstrate how a woman's personal power and magnetism grow when she connects with her feminine essence. When a woman activates this feminine essence, the energy that is in her body and around her moves differently than when she is in her masculine essence. In this chapter you'll discover that without a solid understanding of the biological, emotional, and spiritual make-up of men and women, it is often very difficult to sustain relationships.

Chapter 5—Providing the Food: Exploring Masculine Energy

Chapter 5 naturally flows from exploring the feminine energy to exploring the balance of the yang, masculine energy. The hunter, provider, and protector will be introduced here as the metaphorical provider of food for the table. This chapter will continue to explore the roles of both energies, identifying the core need of the masculine. Through this exploration you'll find out why women test their men—and yes, they should be teaching this information in schools—and you'll also learn the three key words that every masculine archetype needs to hear.

Chapter 6—Saying Grace: The Power of Gratitude

A prayer of grace is an act of giving thanks and a blessing that sanctifies a meal. Chapter 6 mirrors this practice to explore the power of gratitude and appreciation. The reality is that men and women have different needs, and in order to keep love and fulfillment alive, you must acknowledge these needs in a space of appreciation. This chapter details the importance of adopting an attitude of gratitude and explores strategies for understanding and celebrating the differences between males and females. The key purpose here is to create a connection based on mutual trust and understanding.

Chapter 7—Feeding Our Bodies: The Seasons of Intimacy

It's time to eat. The food on the kitchen table depends on the seasons and the natural flow of what the planet is producing—strawberries in the summer, oranges in the winter. Chapter 7 explores the seasonal flow of your love life. Just as seasons have certain characteristics, your relationships also experience a cycle defined by certain traits and core needs. There is a flow in everything you do. While Mother Earth gives you clues and dictates the food for your table, your body also experiences cycles of intimacy against the backdrop of your relationship cycle. Awareness of these cycles is incredibly powerful and allows you to choose to self-regulate your actions based on a sound understanding of your own seasonal flow.

Chapter 8—Dinner Conversation: The Power of Communication

The table is set with the fruits of your labour. You've said grace, and now it's time to enjoy the meal. In chapter 8 you'll learn about the power of the dinner conversation as a metaphor for general communication in a relationship. Your words create your emotions, which then create your actions. From your actions flow the results you are getting in your life right now. Want better results? This chapter is filled with simple tips to articulate your words and style of communication more powerfully. You'll discover the power of language and communication models that reveal the inside secrets on what your lover is *really* thinking.

Chapter 9—Temptation for Dessert: Keeping Sexual Desire Alive

In cultures around the world dessert or pudding is a course that typically comes at the end of a meal, usually consisting of sweet food. For some it's a nightly ritual, while for others it's a rare treat. Chapter 9 will take the symbol of dessert as a metaphor for sexual intimacy, exploring the power of temptation and defining what role you currently play in the bedroom. This final section in the nine-step metaphor is literally the cherry on the top. You'll delve into a discussion on the power of the physical body and how to leverage sexual archetypes. You'll explore juicy topics ranging from the art of seduction to inside knowledge on what he or she *really* wants in the bedroom.

How to Read This Book

Each new discovery throughout this book will combine to increase your ability to have fulfilling relationships. While the structure allows you to flip to relevant chapters based on your immediate desire for knowledge, my intention is that you should read this book front to back. A picnic-rug-style dinner on the floor is fun for a Friday movie night, yet in reality it's not sustainable. You need to create a space to eat that's built on a solid foundation.

You must create a tabletop with a solid base and strong legs as a symbol for relationship beliefs. Next there must be a guiding light that sets the atmosphere for love to thrive, driven by a hierarchy of values. Basic tools are then required to hunt, gather, and prepare the food, drawing on a balance of both masculine and feminine energy. The flow of the seasons dictates what food sources are available to you right now and mirrors everyday cycles of intimacy. Once these primary needs are met, you can experience a more intellectual level of communication through conversation, the freedom of choice, and the molding of your desires through your saying of grace. You can then be rewarded for the fruits of your labour with temptation for dessert, and you can experience a physical and emotional level of intimacy based on your own blueprint of phenomenal love. Ultimately by working through the steps of the model, you'll be creating your own version and blueprint for what *Love on the Kitchen Table* means to you.

The order of the steps in the model is equally important. If you have limiting beliefs about relationships—the structure of your table—then the rest of the theories are irrelevant, as they have no solid foundation upon which to rest. For example, if some part of you truly believes that "it's all downhill after marriage" or that "true love never lasts," then you'll constantly be seeking reference points to support these beliefs. You will manifest examples that reinforce your beliefs because this is what your unconscious mind is searching for.

So who's blueprint of a successful relationship are you going to follow? Are you going to allow yourself to get trapped by the dogma of other people's thinking? Are you going to buy into the jelly bean theory and truly believe that after marriage there is no more sex? Or are you going to back yourself to create your own blueprint on what it means to have a successful relationship and allow your incredible journey to serve as an example to others?

This book is for those who are committed and open to creating a relationship based on true love and understanding. Those people who will truly get value from this book understand that love is a verb. In order to experience it, you must do it more often. The insights in this book are not a quick fix to eliminate all problems. Instead, the nine steps outlined in the chapters to follow provide a guide of information, but you must still take action as part of your own journey. I cannot live it for you. In order for this to be a win-win situation, you must make a commitment to success. Otherwise the information in this book is purely words on a page, and you will continue to be led by the beliefs of the majority. Instead, in order to read on, you must be ready to commit *yes* to the following three questions:

1. Is your relationship with yourself and with your significant other worth investing in?
2. Are you 100 per cent committed to creating even more loving, fulfilling, and empowering connections right now?

3. And most importantly, are you going to back yourself 100 per cent of the way?

There will be challenges. It will not all be smooth sailing, and there will be times when you will need to speak out against the crowd to support your beliefs and back your commitment to happiness. Other individuals will be looking for cracks. They will be looking to fault your approach and will take comfort in your struggles to reinforce their own beliefs that there is no such thing as a happy relationship. Whose blueprint are you going to follow?

With intent must come action. I once read that you should not pick up another book until you have integrated at least five things into your daily life that you have learnt from the book you just read. Otherwise it all becomes shelf help. Personal insights on growth simply rest on the shelf to collect dust while you get caught up in the whirlwind of life without actually committing to action and change. When I learnt this simple strategy, things began to truly shift in my life. I sought new information and then followed through on creating small steps of action and change. The important thing to note here is the power of the small steps. The energy associated with imagining your life as a journey of never-ending improvement is extremely powerful. Constantly looking for improvements, no matter how small, fuels opportunities to lift your personal standards to create your desired, high-quality life. If you define your success as a journey rather than an end destination, then you can take comfort that personal growth and satisfaction can come from constant and never-ending improvement. Rome really wasn't built in a day. Instead, the magnificence of the city is a combination of rock upon rock upon rock. Each pavement segment needed to be laid in order for the next to follow.

Like these paved segments, this book seeks to share the insights that have taken Hayden and my relationship from great to phenomenal, not because everything is now perfect but because we now have an increased understanding around what it means to have a successful relationship based on our own terms. We can now *do* love more often rather than wait for it to fall from the fairy-tale sky. The ideal relationship doesn't come packaged on your doorstep. Instead, great results take great action. We have built a solid foundation and value our metaphoric kitchen table as the heart of our home. And most importantly, we are committed to a continued journey of growth together.

German physicist and philosopher Werner Heisenberg once said that when we observe something; both the observer and the observed are changed. What this means is that your life must change in some form based on your simple decision to read the contents of this book. As you feed your mind valuable insights on how to create relationship success, there must be a shift in the level of your thinking transpired through your emotions and into the results you achieve because when you start looking at your relationship, you as well as your relationship are changed. This is the exciting news. The extent to which you take it is now up to you.

The pages of this book will equip you to create your own blueprint for a successful relationship. As you read, commit to the areas where you will choose to take immediate action in your own life right now because action will make all the difference. It's not the humble structure of the kitchen table that makes it the heart of a family home. Rather, it's the relationships that are built upon its surface and the moments we experience in its presence. These intangible experiences are created over time through a living, breathing journey of love. This is where the magic exists. When you are clear on what a successful relationship means to you, you can then commit to creating a lifelong journey of relationship success. Watch as your world begins to shift. This is my gift to you.

My mission is simple. May more people choose to embrace happy relationships. May more people be proud to speak out on the success of a connection that transcends all barriers. May the ripple effect of love see the frequency of divorce decrease and the numbers of happy marriages increase. Relationships are at the core of everything we do. Our world deserves more happy relationships.

Chapter 1

Building the Table: Beliefs as the Foundation of a Relationship

Beliefs are your foundation,
and everything else takes place because of them.
They are strong, convincing, and highly influential.

What if you were to acknowledge that all the beliefs you have about the world around you are simply made up, chosen by you as a result of your past experiences? I want you to hold this thought for a moment, put the book down, and just ponder this concept for as long as you need. It requires you to let go of a lot of things. It requires you to take responsibility for the way in which your world appears. Total responsibility.

You see, the world is like a dream where the truths of the world are an alluring illusion based on what you choose to see. It's like we each wear an invisible pair of glasses and see the world through the lenses of past experiences—made up of your beliefs, your values, and your way of interpreting your world around you. No one person's pair of glasses is the same as the next, and therefore we all see a different version of reality. There is no truth, only your perception through your unique set of lenses.

If you are slightly uncomfortable right now or even a little confused, please trust the process and allow the confusion to exist. It's a good thing. It means you are stepping outside of your comfort zone, which can then lead to growth. It means you are allowing your mind to consider new possibilities, and in the space of new thinking, new results become possible. This is the entire intent of this book. My purpose is to shift your thinking in terms of the way you approach both your life and your most intimate relationship. An exploration on the fundamental structure of beliefs is where the shift in thinking begins. Often we are led to believe that events control our lives and that our environment has shaped who we are today. Yet this is far from the truth. It's not the events of your life that shape you but your beliefs as to what those events mean and the consequent meanings you choose to carry forward. You are the creator of your beliefs based on your interpretation of your experiences. You then use your beliefs to support you in navigating your world through the lenses of your perception. It is essential you understand this concept on some level. Throughout the book I will be highlighting important concepts such as this one through pop-out text like the example that follows. I encourage you to take note of these statements so you can easily revisit them as needed to support your own journey of growth.

**It's not the events of your life that shape you
but your beliefs as to what those events mean.**

This book must begin here. It must begin with a discussion and reflection on your own beliefs about relationships, love, commitment, and marriage. The single greatest obstacle you face when it comes to your relationship is your own attitude and belief about what things mean. From the day you were born you've been taught basic tenets about what it means to be in a relationship. From your family network, wider community, and global landscape, you've been bombarded with mixed messages. It was this mixed messaging that had me so confronted and confused when Hayden and I first got engaged. While part of me was committed to marriage, another part was challenged by the reactions and responses to our engagement. What this signaled was that my own beliefs around love, commitment, and marriage were not strong enough to back me in my actions and thinking. In fact, when we first got engaged, I had never taken the time to explore my own beliefs around these topics, so the discussion on beliefs had not registered on my conscious radar yet. The reality was I had no clear idea on what love, commitment, and marriage truly meant to me. The Irish rock band The Script sum the danger of this situation up perfectly in their lyrics from their hit song "Fall For Anything": "You've got to stand for something or you'll fall for anything." I wasn't clear on what I stood for and therefore was truly open to falling for anything. Would the jelly bean jar ever get emptied? Was fun travel off the agenda for all married couples? Was it really downhill after the walk down the aisle?

Society is filled with vast and varied viewpoints on relationships, and given the prevalent patterns of divorce, many of these viewpoints are negative. I would argue it is harder to be in a happy, fulfilling relationship today than it used to be. Being in a happy relationship or a fulfilling marriage requires a climate that's supportive of this goal, and often this reality is not so. Instead, we are faced with challenges from society that question our happiness and isolate us in our thinking.

The underlying problem is not with love, commitment, and marriage but instead with our individual attitudes towards these themes. The key question is this: What meaning do you *choose* to give each of these concepts, and what direct impact does that then have on your life and relationships? And more importantly, *whose* attitudes and beliefs are you adopting? Are your beliefs congruent to the results you desire, or on an unconscious level are you in fact trapped by dogma and living with the results of other people's thinking? Are roadblocks stopping you from achieving true happiness and fulfillment in your relationships?

Once accepted, our beliefs become automatic commands to our nervous systems. What we think about comes about, and our thoughts lead the way to a self-fulfilling prophecy. Therefore, if we want to actively influence the results in our lives, then we must take conscious control over our beliefs. This means understanding what they really are and how they are formed. I can share with you all the insights I've learnt during my research and journey to date, yet if you have underlying limiting beliefs around love, commitment, or marriage—as part of what it means to be in a relationship—then the insights shared in this book will fall on deaf ears.

Beliefs truly are the foundation for the kitchen table. Represented by the symbol of the tabletop and supporting legs, everything else happens around them and because of them. They are strong, convincing, and highly influential.

What Is a Belief?

Beliefs are intangible. They are simply a feeling of certainty about what something means. If you say you believe in love at first sight, all you are really saying is this: "I feel *certain* that love at first sight exists." This feeling of certainty then allows you to tap into resources that exist within you to produce results that reinforce your belief—in this case, "love at first sight." All possibilities exist within you, yet often your lack of certainty means you are unable to access your potential and bring desired possibilities to fruition.

All possibilities exist within you.

Self-help author and motivational speaker Anthony Robbins says the simple way of understanding this concept together with the structure of beliefs is to think about the basic building block— an idea. There are lots of ideas you may think about but not really believe. For example, take the idea that you are worthy of love and say to yourself, "I am completely worthy of love." Now whether this is an idea or a belief will come down to the level of certainty you feel about this statement. If a part of you is not congruent with the idea or a small voice in your head is whispering, "No you're not," then all this really means is that you don't feel very *certain* that you are worthy of love. This makes the concept an idea as opposed to a deep-set belief that you feel certain about.

So how do you turn an idea into a belief? Inspired by Anthony Robbins and his work on beliefs in *Awaken the Giant Within,* a simple tabletop metaphor can be used to clearly explain the concept of beliefs and as an appropriate beginning for the magic to follow as part of the *Love on the Kitchen Table* model. The beliefs table metaphor requires you to think of an idea as a tabletop with no supporting legs. Without the supporting legs, the tabletop is flat on the ground with nothing to support it. On the other hand, a *belief* is a tabletop with supporting legs. These legs act as reference points that tell you the belief is true. The legs, as reference points, increase the level of certainty and reinforce the belief to form a solid structure. The more reference points, the stronger the belief. As an example, the following diagram illustrates the belief that "it's all downhill after marriage." The legs of the table then illustrate the reference points that support this particular belief. Examples of reference points, as perceived by an individual, may include the following:

Divorce rates are high, so something must go wrong at some stage.

My parents are divorced and seem happier on their own.

My best friend got married, and now she never goes out or has fun anymore. In fact, she spends the majority of her time complaining about her life.

Belief table with example reference points

These reference points have no real significance on their own until they are organised under the belief that "it's all downhill after marriage." Once connected to this overarching concept, they then work to solidify the idea and increase the associated levels of certainty. When an idea is supported by certainty it then becomes a belief. Each belief has its own set of reference points, and the more reference points you have to support a certain belief, the stronger it becomes. You can develop a belief about anything, providing you have enough reference points to support the idea as a belief through high levels of certainty.

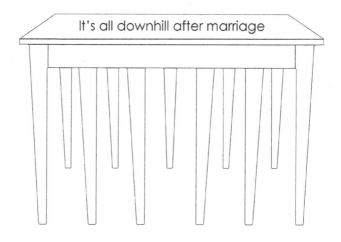

It's all downhill after marriage

As a belief becomes stronger, the automatic commands to your nervous system are increased, and you begin to delete, distort, and generalise information so that you are only taking in what your mind is searching for. The brain loves consistency, and it constantly works to make order of chaos. It will search for evidence for what it perceives to be true based on your perceptions and beliefs of the world. The brain will automatically look for reference points to support the tabletop and further reinforce the belief. In order for change work and transformation to take place, the overarching belief must be addressed, as opposed to addressing only the specific details of the reference points.

A belief can be described as your best explanation of the world based on your current evidence. You have thousands of beliefs, the majority of which you are not even aware of, that direct the results you experience. Some of these beliefs support you in creating the results you desire while other beliefs hold you back and even sabotage your efforts. As a general example, one person may have the belief that "life is hard" while another person may believe that "life is an adventure." Imagine how you might compare the ways in which these two people are going to experience their world around them. Imagine how these beliefs may impact their relationships with others, including their most intimate partner. Ultimately, based on these two diverse beliefs, these people are going to experience very different models of the world. As another example, the feeling of certainty, or belief around "love at first sight," can be explored further in terms of achieving relationship goals. If you are looking to find a lifelong partner, then this belief may support you in achieving that goal more easily and effortlessly, as it allows you to be open to an extended range of possibilities. Alternatively if you believe that "love takes time to achieve and needs to be developed over a period of time through trials and tribulations," then your experience of finding love may be very different to the version that believes in love at first sight. The key point here is that neither of the beliefs is right or wrong. Exploring beliefs is not about asking whether a belief is true or not. Rather, the exploration of beliefs is about asking the key question: "Is this belief I currently have nurturing, serving, and supporting me right now to achieve my desired outcomes? Or is this belief holding me back?"

Beliefs and Relationships

Beliefs are the building blocks for the way in which we experience our world, and they have a profound impact on the way we choose to experience love and relationships. Many relationships today are crumbling because they lack a sturdy and strong foundation based on solid relationship beliefs about love and commitment.

I worked with an incredible woman who was experiencing relationship challenges. She felt her partner was constantly absorbed in his own life, spending very little time with her and more concerned with working, making money, having a social life, and playing sports. She also felt disconnected with what it would mean to experience a strong, trusting, and loving relationship. A part of her knew it was not about her man but rather a familiar cycle she was witnessing in her history of relationships with men in general. The same part of her knew that if she were to end the relationship and seek a loving connection elsewhere, she would continue to experience the same emotions relating to a lack of love, appreciation, and trust. Yet she couldn't quite put her finger on exactly what was missing.

We worked together to explore her beliefs around men, love, and marriage. Not surprisingly at the heart of the exploration her core beliefs were obvious barriers to her ability to experience love. She believed the following: "Men are selfish. Love is challenging, and marriage is doomed for divorce." The results in her life were a direct reflection of these beliefs and a self-fulfilling prophecy guided by the fundamental thoughts present in her unconscious mind. Together we explored the reference points—the legs of the belief table—that told her these beliefs were true. Her relationship was experiencing challenges because of her perceived lack of love and consequent anger towards her man's focus on external elements, including his work, finances, friends, and sports. Each of these examples was a solid reference point that reinforced her beliefs. When her man chose to go to the gym after work rather than come straight home to see her, this supported her belief that "men are selfish." When he chose to see his friends once a week, again she chose to make this a reference point that supported the same selfish association with men. She had experienced similar challenges in previous relationships, so naturally this evidence point reinforced to her that "love is challenging," another one of her overarching beliefs. She had no plans to commit long term through marriage, as she couldn't understand why she would put herself in a situation that she believed would lead to heartache and divorce based on her belief that "all marriages are doomed for divorce."

We broke this third belief down even further to analyse the reference points that reinforced the sense of certainty behind this belief. Not surprisingly she talked about her parent's messy divorce, which is a primary reference point that often triggers limiting beliefs around marriage for many youth growing up in a split-marriage environment. She also discussed other relationship challenges she had witnessed with family and friends close to her, and when prompted, she was unable to name a single couple she knew who were happily married. Through this acknowledgement of the vast amount of reference points supporting her limiting beliefs around men, love, and commitment, she realised the immense impact these beliefs were having on the results she was getting in her life at that moment. She also realised that even if she were to end the relationship and move on to the next man, the same challenges would quickly emerge. The challenge was in the way she was *viewing* the problem, as opposed to the perceived problem itself. Her limiting beliefs were completely stopping her from achieving her desire to have a happy and fulfilling relationship.

꧁꧂

The way you see the problem
is the problem.

꧁꧂

Another young married woman talks to her friends about marriage. "I'd always had this feeling that if you got married, it was like the end of who you are. Well, I'm married now, so I'll see how it goes." Not surprisingly three years following the time the woman made this statement, she was now divorced. Having a negative attitude towards commitment and marriage beforehand creates a self-fulfilling prophecy that presupposes the end. Entering into a marriage believing it will be the end of who you are prevents you from making the emotional investment necessary to produce a successful marriage.

The Buddhist principle sums this concept up perfectly. *All that we are is the result of what we have thought.* The mind is everything. What we think we become. We can continue to develop this level of thinking further as we reflect on our attitudes towards certain topics. For example, divorce in modern society is accepted in a much different form than it was fifty years ago. In terms of "what we think we become," a detrimental attitude that is harmful when one is entering into a marriage is the idea that presupposes you can simply get a divorce when things go wrong. The issue with this level of thinking and the beliefs that support this thinking imply that one's approach often determines the outcome. Barry Schwartz in *The Paradox of Choice* wrote,

> The very option of being allowed to change our minds seems to increase the chances we *will* change our minds. When we can change our minds about decisions, we are less satisfied with them. Alternatively, when a decision is final, we engage in a variety of psychological processes that enhance our feelings about the choice we made relative to the alternatives.

With this in mind, for many people the option of knowing you can easily and effortlessly get a divorce provides comfort and support. Why is this comfort required? What real challenges are being suppressed by this perceived get-out-of-jail-free card? Ultimately at the core of this level of thinking there are underlying beliefs that are not conducive to a successful marriage, and it is here where the real thinking and change work must focus.

The Imprinting Phase and Defining Moments

When you are born, you are like a blank canvas. While on some level the canvas has already been created and pulled tight over its wooden frame, the coloured artwork of life is yet to be created. All that exists is pure and white. It is clean. It is fresh. It is completely open and vulnerable. Based on what you experience, you then choose to add meaning or feelings of certainty to everything you interpret in your world. These ideas and feelings of certainty then form your beliefs and become the artwork of the life you choose to live.

NLP is an approach to communication, personal development, and psychotherapy created in the 1970s by Richard Bandler and John Grinder. As part of this study of human behaviour, the imprinting phase is referenced as the period between birth and seven years when the majority of your beliefs are formed. During this time you learn all you can about the world at a rapid rate. You experience events and choose to give them a meaning based on what you know and perceive you experience at that time. You develop beliefs about what you perceive things mean, and these beliefs then guide you throughout your life. NLP developer and author Robert Dilts defines an imprint as "a significant experience or period of life from the past in which a person formed a belief, or cluster of beliefs, often in relationship to one's identity." To put this in to context, imagine the five-year-old girl who is dressed as a fairy, playing make-believe in a magical space that is her fairy-tale bedroom. She frolics between her bed and her pile of toys, waving her magical wand and fluffing her pink tutu, the perfect match to her pink singlet top, tiara, and silver glittery shoes. Her wings are attached with tight elastic, and she's got her stylish sequined handbag at the ready. Yet playtime is quickly over when

Mum arrives and sternly expresses her concern. "What are you doing? We are running late to visit Grandma, and there is no time for this rubbish. Get dressed and let's get going. Now," she snaps. In that moment the five-year-old girl shrinks from her make-believe land and feels naughty and wrong. She tells herself there is no time for playfulness and feeling pretty and quickly gets dressed to go to Grandma's. The seed for the belief that "there is no time for playfulness and feeling pretty" has been planted, and as part of the imprinting phase this belief becomes rooted to a connection and feeling of sadness connected to self-love. The connection to sadness is important to note because while our memory gives us the ability to recall specific events from the past, our ability to recall the details of these events accurately is difficult, and instead we find it easiest to access the emotions that were associated with the event at the time. For example, if you recall a favourite memory or experience, notice how the feelings of joy and happiness are close by. While the specific details of the event may be a little blurry, the associated emotions can be easily accessed. Notice what you saw. Hear what you heard and feel the intense feeling of the moment. As another example, recall a moment that caused you great sorrow and notice how the feelings of sadness are close by. See what you saw, hear what you heard, and feel the intense feelings of the moment. In the example of the five-year-old girl, she chose to connect her experience to sadness as the emotion that was triggered as part of the event. With the

16

belief that "there is no time for playfulness and feeling pretty" connected to feelings of sadness around self-love, what results do you think this little girl is now experiencing as a woman of thirty-six years of age? More specifically, what results do you think she is getting in her relationships in terms of how she approaches love and feels about her role within an intimate connection?

One event can plant the seed to shape an entire life. Yet what must be acknowledged is that this is the meaning this young girl *chose* to give this event. Another child may have thought nothing of the comment from Mum and continued on a fairy-tale vision as part of the adventure to Grandma's house. Again it is essential to note that it's not the event itself that creates the beliefs but rather the meaning that becomes associated with the event. It's never the environment or the events of your life that shape you but the meaning you attach to the events and how you interpret them. It is the meaning and interpretations you choose that shape who you are today and who you'll become tomorrow.

**One event can plant the seed
to shape an entire life.**

While my intention has been to highlight negative beliefs and defining moments as catalysts for change, defining moments can also be positive and influence your decisions in ways that empower you. As you explore your own beliefs and defining moments as part of the exercise at the end of this chapter, you might also like to acknowledge and celebrate the specific milestones and events during your imprinting period that have had a positive impact on your life in terms of developing a belief that has served you. One event can shape an entire future without you consciously realising it, yet when you work to bring the belief into your conscious awareness, that's when you can reflect upon the real power of the event and associated belief. Ask yourself, "Is this belief nurturing, serving, and supporting me right now to achieve my desired outcomes?" If the answer is no, you can work to acknowledge the history of the belief, thank the belief for the role it has played to date, and then say farewell to the belief in order to create space for new, more empowering beliefs that will better serve you moving forward. The process for changing beliefs is explored later in this chapter, but for now let's take a look at our changing landscape.

A Changing Landscape

In their book *The Flipside of Feminism* Suzanne Venker and Phyllis Schlafly claim that many people today have no idea *how* to be married or even how to go about choosing the right spouse. They quote two reasons for this occurrence. Firstly today's youth are being raised in a culture that refuses to embrace the unique natures of males and females, creating a zone characterised by power struggles, conflict, and strain. Secondly most young people have been either directly or indirectly affected by divorce, which has led to distrust and negative associations with marriage. While it is important to reflect on our own defining moments as part of our childhood and the influence of our primary role models, it is also important to zoom out and look at the bigger shifts within society as a whole, reflecting on how these shifts may also be impacting the meaning we give certain themes.

Since the 1960s divorce rates have increased by more than 100 per cent, and the total amount of people getting married has decreased by 45 per cent. We have more divorces and less people getting married than ever before; and with this in mind, it's interesting to note the other relevant events that have been happening during this time. Of particular interest in terms of the impact on relationships is the rise of feminism—the second-wave feminist movement began in the 1960s, coinciding with the timing in the sharp rise in divorce numbers.

As a brief historical overview, feminism has three distinct classifications:

1. First wave—nineteenth-century suffragettes
2. Second wave—1960s feminists
3. Third wave—today's feminists, preferring the term "women's movement"

Venker and Schlafly stress the importance of noting the key differences between the first-wave feminist movement (suffragettes) and the second-wave feminism (1960s), arguing that the two movements had very little in common. The suffragettes were members of the National Union of Women's Suffrage Societies, which was founded in 1897 as a collection of local suffrage societies. Suffragettes were mostly women from upper- and middle-class backgrounds, frustrated by their social and economic situation. The key milestone of the first-wave feminist movement was the fight for the right for woman to vote, a fight that was won when New Zealand become the first self-governing country to grant woman the right to vote in parliamentary elections in 1893. While oppression was a key driver in this first-wave feminist movement, the suffragettes remained family orientated and had no desire to eradicate female nature.

In contrast, the second-wave feminist movement, which kicked off in the 1960s, had a very different approach in its positioning of the core family network. The shift from moral obligation to self-fulfillment saw women choosing a life outside of the family home as a means of liberation from the traps of family life. What we began to see in the 1960s second-wave feminist movement was a rejection and rebellion from what it meant to live life as a female. In her book *The Feminist Mystique,* key activist and feminist from the second-wave women's movement Betty Friedan argues that a woman's devotion to her husband and children is a sacrifice of such magnitude that it inevitably stunts her growth as an individual. She argues that time in the home is a thankless pursuit that doesn't allow women to use their intelligence in a manner that benefits society. The common beliefs of this time period were "housewives are bored" and "being a mother stunts your growth." These beliefs were delivered on mass, and as a result, we saw a surge of woman breaking free from the perceived constraints of motherhood to take up high-powered careers in a search for fulfillment outside of the home. At the same time we began to see a rejection of males and a shift towards thinking that women could do it all on their own—downgrading the role of males in both society and within the dynamics of a relationship. "In the span of just a few decades, women have managed to demote men from respected providers and protectors to being unnecessary, irrelevant, and expendable," writes Venker and Schlafly.

As part of the 1960s feminist movement, the focus shifted to an individual pursuit for power, ultimately having a profound and detrimental impact on the state of our relationships. Married couples no longer thought of themselves as one unit but instead as separate entities sharing space, leading to an obscuring of gender roles and inevitable conflict as each spouse focused solely on his or her needs rather than the needs of the relationship. Author William Powers sums up the accumulative affect following this shift in thinking, for "when a crowd adopts a point of view en masse, all critical thinking stops."

I strongly feel that a close reflection on the feminist movement illustrates the force-feeding of society's beliefs or the force-feeding of the beliefs of the elite, who have the ability to control the messages we see in the media. This shift in focus for mass-fed beliefs then in turn determines the perceived meaning of fundamental themes, such as what it means to be a man or woman. Consider the characteristics I've touched on as part of the 1960s feminist movement where the structures of society and men were blamed for the perceived suppression of females. The belief that "women are oppressed" began to litter entertainment media, books, movies, the workplace, and public school systems. The solution was the rejection of the feminine and a vicious drive towards a sexless society, where all individuals were positioned as equals. This approach disregarded the spiritual power and balance of masculine and feminine energy and instead moved our society to an ever-increasing masculine state of competition for sameness.

Venker and Schlafly claim feminism has been the single worst thing that has happened to women, and while I don't necessarily agree with the finality of this statement, I definitely feel it is worth consideration in terms of the impact feminism has had on our individual belief systems. Venker and Schlafly argue that feminism did not liberate women at all but instead confused them, creating a conflict between man and nature. They claim,

> Their female nature tells them sex requires love;
> marriage is important; children are a blessing; and

men are necessary. The culture, meanwhile, tells them to sleep around and postpone family life because that will cost them their identity. And, if their marriage doesn't work out, it's no big deal. They can always get divorced.

It is here where I believe the confusion is warranted, where many women are caught up in tangled webs of beliefs about what it means to be a woman, wife, and mother.

Of particular note is a belief that evolved on a cultural level that implies fulfillment for women can only be sought outside of the family home. Yet in reality this is not the case for everyone, and many women find fulfillment in caring for and nurturing a strong family unit. The point is that your reaction to marriage, motherhood, and what it means to be a woman must be based on your *own* set of beliefs, goals, and vision for your life. Anyone can feel bored or trapped at virtually any job. It is how one chooses to respond to boredom that is key. It is the fundamental beliefs at play that really need to be reviewed, and the essential question to ask yourself is the following: Are your beliefs truly yours and in alignment with your values, or are they based on the perceived norms of society?

Living in a culture where divorce is accepted by society makes it challenging to stay married, but it's even harder when divorce is glorified. My intent in reflecting on a changing landscape is not to challenge the decision over the role of working mothers versus stay-at-home parenting or marriage versus cohabitation but to instead spark a new level of thinking in your own thought system to ensure the beliefs you have about these topics are congruent to your own self-image.

**Are your beliefs in alignment with *your* values,
or are they based on the perceived
norms of society?**

The current divorce statistics cannot be viewed in a void and must instead be reflected upon in terms of a changing landscape. Once you can step back and take a look at the patterns in society and understand their impact on mass thinking, then you are better placed to reflect on your own attitudes and beliefs. Ultimately the decisions on how you choose to live your life must be congruent with who you are, including the goals and dreams you desire in the context of your own map of reality.

How to Change Limiting Beliefs

So far in this chapter we've covered the definition of what exactly a belief is, the profound impact beliefs have on guiding the results in your life, the impact of beliefs on relationships, the birthing of beliefs during the imprinting phase from birth to seven years, and the importance of acknowledging a changing landscape, particularly where new beliefs are delivered on mass. While you are reading these sections, it is likely you are already beginning to reflect on your own belief system. You may have already identified beliefs that are holding you back, and you may have had ideas for new beliefs that will better serve you moving forward. This final section, as part of the beliefs chapter, now works to put all the previous learning together in a simple five-step format that can create life-changing results.

Creating new beliefs that are in alignment with who we want to be can be challenging for some people, especially if the old pattern is strongly rooted over many years of practice. I worked with a lady on some relationship challenges she was experiencing as part of a longer pattern of resistance to commitment. When we first began our work together, she was engaged to be married, yet she was experiencing intense internal conflicts around commitment and the impact she perceived marriage would have on her life. As a result, she was creating relationship challenges as a form of self-sabotage. Her map of the world told her that when you get married you lose your self-worth. Her underlying belief was that "marriage means loss of self." She had many reference points that supported this belief, including her mother and primary role model, who had suppressed her own needs for happiness over the years in order to serve her family. She also had a close friend who had recently separated from her husband and said it was the greatest thing she'd ever done. Returning to the tabletop analogy, the more reference points and supporting legs a belief has, the stronger the belief becomes and the more challenging it may be to change. Yet those people who are completely committed to creating new results can choose more empowering beliefs and build them up to be equally as strong. The key is to bust down the supporting legs of the limiting belief and instead build up the supporting legs of the more empowering belief. It's about following the steps, backing yourself, and then celebrating the process as you move forward. There are five key stages to changing a limiting belief, and I will work through this particular client's challenges in order to give you a reference frame for understanding each of the steps.

While you may like to take notes as you read or highlight particular points of relevance, a full exercise for your own exploration is included at the end of this chapter. My suggestion is to read these next sections with the intent to understand the concepts and to then work through each of the steps in more detail when you get to the "Exercises for Reflection" section at the end.

Step 1: Identify a limiting belief.

Identifying a limiting belief is the first step in the process of becoming able to change it. Beliefs, as a feeling of certainty, are often anything that come after the words *I am*— or *Something is*—. For example, an exploration on your beliefs around relationships would begin by completing your responses to the following sentences:

- Love is—
- Commitment is—
- Marriage is—

The defining moments exercise detailed earlier in this chapter can also be used to identify limiting beliefs by exploring the moment when the belief first began to develop during the imprinting phase. As you work to put together a list of the beliefs you would like to change, remember that there is no right or wrong, only what is true for you. Based on your own perception, if your current belief does not support you in reaching your desired outcomes, then it is limiting you in realising your full potential.

Example: For the purpose of this exercise, we will work with the limiting belief that "marriage means loss of self" to demonstrate how we might then work to change the belief.

Step 2: Choose a belief you would like to have instead.

I often think acknowledgement is 90 per cent of the journey. Once you get to the core of what is going on and acknowledge that change needs to take place in order to achieve new results, then you are already changing. From here you then get to focus on choosing new ways of doing things. Once you have identified a limiting belief that you would like to change, the next step is to select a new, more empowering belief. If you find that coming up with a new belief is challenging, ask yourself what you would tell someone you cared about if they were in the same situation? What would you want a child to believe?

Example: Rather than the belief that "marriage means loss of self," a more empowering belief might be "marriage is a beautiful and supportive partnership that allows you to grow, develop, and further discover your own unique sense of being."

Step 3: Acknowledge the emotional payoff.

Once you have identified your limiting belief and selected a new, more empowering one, the third step is to acknowledge how the limiting belief has served you over the years. And yes, it has served you. When I ask my clients this question, they often respond by saying, "It hasn't. How could this belief possibly serve me?" Yet the essential thing to note is that the brain is wired to serve you in the best way it knows how. You must therefore accept that your beliefs, even the ones that you have now identified as limiting, have in fact served you in some form over the years. Most likely they have kept you safe within the comfort zone of your current thinking.

Example: In this case, the emotional payoff of the belief "marriage means loss of self" kept the client safe from getting hurt based on her perceptions and connections with marriage and pain. The belief also allowed her to feel compassion towards her family by sharing the same story as previous family members had perceived it. And finally the belief also met a need for drama by creating relationship challenges to support the belief.

Following the acknowledgement of the emotional payoffs, it is essential to check in and see if these payoffs are worth the decision to hold on to the belief. If the payoffs are serving you, how else will you meet these needs once the belief is gone? In this example the client worked through developing a new story of connection to continue a state of rapport with her family network. It was essential that the new story allowed her to acknowledge her roots yet also empowered her in creating new results. To ensure this continued connection with her family, she chose to reframe her belief to this: "Because of the challenges my family has experienced with their beliefs around marriage, I have become empowered to do things differently and to pave the way for new, more resourceful ways of being married. I am an inspiration for generations to come, and I'm proud of breaking the patterns of divorce and heartache while also respecting my roots."

This shift in thinking allowed her a safe space to change her belief system and still remain connected to the roots of her family network. In terms of the drama payoff, she identified a need for variety and adventure, as served by the drama cycle. When we removed the relationship challenges as a way to meet a need for drama, we then had to fill the void with a more resourceful strategy. My client committed to booking more weekend getaways and more overseas trips with her man as a resourceful way to meet her need for drama and excitement.

Once convinced the emotional payoffs could be achieved in more resourceful ways, she no longer saw a purpose for the belief that "marriage means loss of self" and was ready to let it go completely. At this point I encourage you to hold a farewell ceremony that may involve writing the belief on a piece of paper and then burning the paper or sending a natural item out to sea as a symbolic metaphor of release. Ensure you thank your belief for the way in which it has served you up until this point and also make it clear that you are now ready to move on and adopt new, more empowering beliefs that can better serve you going forward.

Step 4: Reframe the evidence and reference points.

After acknowledging the emotional payoff and saying farewell to the belief, it's then important to address the reference points— the legs of the table that are now left in isolation. Each of the reference points must be reframed to take on a more empowering meaning, which involves rewording the reference points to say it how you want it.

Example

Consider our example:

- **Old reference point:** Mum suppressed her own needs for happiness over the years in order to serve her family, so that must be the way things go.
- **New reframe:** Mum was doing the best should could with the resources she perceived she had. She gifted me with such a solid foundation on which to grow further.

- **Old reference point:** My best friend recently separated from her husband and said it was the greatest thing she'd ever done.
- **New reframe:** My best friend's life is not mine. While I support her as a friend, I choose to notice and model successful relationships based on sustainable love, growth, and strength.

Step 5: Find evidence for your new belief.

Once you have reframed the evidence and reference points from your old belief, it is time to begin creating additional legs for your new tabletop or belief. This final step is about becoming committed to adopting your new belief and embedding it in your everyday life, supported by points of certainty.

Example
Again consider our example:

- **New belief:** Marriage is a beautiful and supportive partnership that allows you to grow, develop, and further discover your own unique sense of being.

Reference points

- My grandparents have been married for fifty years and have a very successful marriage.
- My fiancé is very supportive, and I love him with all my heart.
- Through this journey right now I am growing to discover a new way of doing love more successfully.

Remember, the more reference points and legs of the table you develop, the stronger your sense of certainty will be, and that supports your new belief. The reality is that if you want more love, you must firstly believe it is possible. Perhaps you might choose to have your new belief symbolically represented as a creative screen saver, posted as an image on your office wall, or scripted through words in your journal. All of these options create a daily check-in point of prominence.

**If you want more love,
you must firstly believe it is possible.**

"Things do not change, we change," are the wise words of philosopher and author Henry David Thoreau. With this in mind, you must take control of how you interpret your world and change your beliefs accordingly to ensure they support, nurture, and sustain you in achieving your goals.

Chapter Summary

The quality of your life is not determined by the events that happen in your life. It's not your level of luck or your hard times. It's not your upbringing, family situation, friends, or society. What determines your quality of life is the meaning you choose to give all of these things and the choices you make as a result. This one key insight has the power to totally transform your life should you choose to truly take it on board. The way you see the problem *is* the problem. The only things preventing you from being who you want to be, doing what you want to do, and having what you want to have are the stories you tell yourself about why you can't. In the words of Anthony Robbins, "What we can or cannot do, what we consider possible or impossible, is rarely a function of our true capability. It is more likely a function of our beliefs about who we are." Beliefs are generalisations for what you observe and for the meaning you choose to assign certain patterns in life. They truly are the cornerstone of our thinking and the structural foundation for the *Love on the Kitchen Table* model.

Exercises for Reflection

The best way to embed your learning is to immediately apply what you've read to your own current situation, to maximise change and impact in your life right now. As you explore the *Love on the Kitchen Table* model, each chapter will conclude with a series of exercises that are relevant to the particular chapter. The purpose of these exercises is to best serve you with a tool for education, conspiring for your success always. If you have any questions about the beliefs exercise below, refer to the corresponding sections in the chapter for further details. There are three parts to the following exercise for reflection.

- **Part 1: Identifying Your Relationship Beliefs**
- **Part 2: Exploring Where Your Beliefs Came from**
- **Part 3: Choosing More Empowering Beliefs**

Part 1: Identifying Your Relationship Beliefs

The first step in breaking down limiting beliefs that may be hindering your relationship success is to identify your current beliefs around relationships. Complete the following sentences, detailing as many points as you need to ensure you get all of your thoughts out on paper. Trust what comes up from your unconscious mind immediately rather than attempting to shape your answers to what you would like them to be. Trust that which exists within you right now.

1. Relationships are—
2. Love is—
3. Commitment is—
4. Marriage is—
5. Woman are—
6. Men are—
7. What does being a wife mean to you?
8. What does being a husband mean to you?
9. What does having a family mean to you?
10. What is most important to you? What do you love, and what are you passionate about?

Reflect on your responses to the statements and questions above. Do your identified beliefs support you in your everyday life, or have you noticed some limiting foundations that may be stopping you from reaching your full potential within your relationship?

Part 2: Exploring Where Your Beliefs Came from

Work through the following questions and consider keeping a journal as you brainstorm your thoughts and feelings in response to the twelve questions below.

1. **Identify the event.** Begin by thinking about a time in your own life when you remember feeling intense emotion during the imprinting ages of birth to seven years or up

until twelve years of age if you feel unable to access events from a younger stage. What specific event do you recall?

2. **Describe the event.** How old are you? Where are you as the event occurs? What do you look like? Who is there with you?

3. **Get specific.** What occurs that makes this event a defining moment?

4. **Connect with the emotions.** What emotions are you noticing in this moment?

5. **Understand what developed in your mind.** What are you telling yourself about this event? About yourself? About the other people? What are you telling yourself about what this all means to you?

6. **Identify if it was positive or negative.** What did you give up or surrender in the form of power and self-determination as a consequence of this event—if negative? Alternatively what did you gain and discover about yourself—if positive?

7. **Identify the belief.** What did you decide to believe as a result of this event?

8. **Determine current impact.** What do you tell yourself today as a result of the belief you have held on to? What price are you paying for by holding on to this belief? What consequences are you seeing in your life right now?

9. **Determine future impact.** What price will you pay in one year's time if you hold on to this belief? Three years? Ten years?

10. **Reality check.** Do you think this view of yourself, of the world, or of those around you is accurate?

11. **Decision time.** Now that you are aware of what you have been telling yourself, ask yourself, "Is this pattern or belief going to serve, support, nurture, and challenge me as I live the rest of my life?"

12. **Choose your own direction.** If your belief does not serve, support, nurture, and challenge you, what belief would? What would you encourage a child to believe?

Work through this list of questions for each of your defining moments and aim to explore at least five significant emotional events. While this exercise may take some time, this is where your transformation begins.

As you work through your defining moments, begin putting together a list of empowering beliefs that will support you as you create your extraordinary life and embrace your ideal relationship. Here are a few examples of beliefs from my own exploration work combined with a selection of favourite beliefs from my clients:

- I believe I am worthy of love.
- I believe I am good enough right now.
- I believe I am completely whole.

- I believe I have all the resources I need to create my ideal life.
- I believe I am capable of doing anything I put my mind to.
- I believe I am 100 per cent responsible for my own happiness and that others are responsible for theirs.
- I believe that people are doing the best they can with the resources they have and that if they knew how to do better, they would.
- I believe I am not responsible for other people's happiness and instead choose to show support through courage, compassion, patience, and love.
- I believe marriage is an exciting adventure.
- I believe marriage is unique to each couple and magical in every way.

Part 3: Choosing More Empowering Beliefs

You have now identified key limiting beliefs, acknowledged the defining moments from which they began, and chosen to select beliefs that are more empowering for moving you forward. Next, work through these five steps for embedding your new belief as part of your everyday thinking.

1. Choose a limiting belief that you are 100 per cent committed to changing right now.
2. Choose a new belief that you would like to have instead.

3. Acknowledge the emotional payoff of the limiting belief you are letting go of. How has it served you up until now?

4. Reframe the evidence and reference points of the limiting belief to create a new, more empowering meaning.

5. Find evidence for your new belief to build the reference points of certainty—the legs of your belief table.

Repeat this exercise for as many limiting beliefs as you choose to address.

Chapter 2

Lighting the Candles of Value: Understanding How Values Guide Relationships

Your recipe to happiness: know your values.

Hayden and I walk through the same shopping mall, yet we see a very different view of our surroundings. I notice the fashion and beauty stores and the new Christmas décor, and I can pick a good coffee shop a mile away; Hayden is much more attuned to the electronics department, fitness outlets, and the nearest food court. With so many sensory elements at play in the setting of the mall, each of us deletes, distorts, and generalises specific elements of our surroundings so that we only experience that which is familiar to our own unique map of the world. This means we each have a completely different experience in how we view our surroundings. Essentially we are seeing very different versions of the shopping mall, and we would recall to strangers who have never visited the mall a very different description of what they might look to experience.

What you choose to focus on and what you allow to filter into your reality is based on your top values, even if you are not aware of them. Your values determine your reality. They implicitly determine what you see, the decisions you make, and the actions you follow through on. Every decision you make in life is based on your hierarchy of values, and when you have trouble making a decision or feel a conflict in your decision-making process, this is often because you are experiencing a values conflict. Yet most people are not aware of their values and therefore are unable to put into language what's going on as part of a decision-making process. In this lack of clarity exists ambiguity, where the path is hazy in terms of leading a fulfilling life, and how can you work towards achieving what it is you don't yet know you want?

**Every decision you make in life
is based on your hierarchy of values.**

The secret to success is about getting clear on what it is you want to create in your everyday world. If you want the deepest level of fulfillment in life, you must decide on what your highest values are and then commit to living by these values each and every day. It really is that simple. A client once remarked that it's the recipe to happiness—define your values and then create a life that aligns to these core qualities. Her simple insight is incredibly accurate. In creating a fulfilling relationship with your significant other, the journey must firstly begin with self. What you believe about yourself and the way you treat yourself is the first example to the world on the way you expect to be treated in return.

These first two chapters as part of the *Love on the Kitchen Table* model—Chapter 1: Building the Table and Chapter 2: Lighting the Candles of Value—are the foundation. I can teach you all the human behaviour models in the world related to relationships, yet if your beliefs do not conspire for your relationship success or if you are unaware of the values that drive your daily decision-making process, then your own personal roadblocks will prevent the full engagement and integration of the remaining chapters and valuable insights to follow.

Lighting the candles of value as part of the *Love on the Kitchen Table* model is about knowing what each of you stands for within your relationship and then bringing your unique set of values together to exist with life and light. To support you on your journey, this chapter takes you through a process of exploring exactly what values are, how to elicit your own values, how to create a life in alignment with your values, and how values integrate in the context of a relationship, including a response to the following common question: Do the values for you and your loved one have to be the same in order for love to thrive?

Candles provide the symbolism for this chapter, representing an individual need to shine brightly as your best version of self so that you can then bring an increased sense of light and love to your relationship. Candles have been used for thousands of years as light and to illuminate our celebrations, yet little is known about their origins. In the same sense, as an individual you cannot possibly know all there is to know about your own origins in terms of your lineage line, wider family history, and precisely how you came to be. Yet you can shine in the here and now with a strong glow based on a solid foundation of knowing what you stand for. Candles are no longer man's major source of light, yet they have continued to grow in popularity. Today they symbolise celebration, mark romance, and are used to soothe the senses and decorate our living spaces. Appropriately they cast a warm, soft glow of intimacy for those in the surrounding space to enjoy.

What Are Values?

Values are the emotional states or qualities that we hold high above all others. If you know your values, then you know who you are and exactly what you stand for. Your life becomes owned by you and shaped by you, and this is a state of incredible empowerment.

Values can be defined in two forms—end values and means values. End values are the emotional states you want to experience, while means values are the vehicles by which you choose to experience these emotional states. When we are talking about values in the context of creating an extraordinary life and relationship success, we are referring to end values, which detail those emotional states you want to experience as part of your ideal world. For example, if you said you value money, I would ask you, "What does money give you?" You might say, "Wealth." I would then ask you, "What does wealth give you?" You might say, "Security." Here you reach a much deeper insight to the true value you are working to achieve. In this sense, the means values are money and wealth while your end value, the deeper value, is security.

What happens in life is that we often get caught up in the material means to achieving our true values. We collect a house, car, and clothes, make a bunch of friends, and tick a few travel boxes, yet what we don't realise is the exact extent to which these items do or don't meet our true values—our end values.

Have you ever experienced the feeling of achieving something you thought you wanted and then reached your outcome only to realise it's not quite what you thought it was going to be. I remember finishing university with my first degree, a bachelor of communications majoring in public relations. At that time I set a goal to get a job at a local agency and reach a certain pay threshold. I worked really hard and focused on the achievement of that goal, yet when I reached it just two years later, I realised it wasn't about the agency or money at all. Instead, I realised it was about a need to meet my career values, which upon further reflection involved a deep-set yearning to serve others (contribution value) and a desire to create choice defined through wealth as opposed to being defined by a salary package (wealth creation value).

**When you know your values, your life becomes
owned by you and shaped by you.**

The power of realising your values will lead to a more fulfilled existence where your life will finally begin to make sense because you know what it is you are working to achieve. I've outlined a list of end values to encourage your thinking around the specific things you value. As you read through the list, note the values that resonate most. This list may help you to define your values as part of the exercise at the end of this chapter—Exercise: Defining Your Values.

- love
- connection
- security
- health
- vitality
- creativity

- passion
- adventure
- wealth creation
- wisdom
- playfulness
- spirituality
- religion
- gratefulness
- freedom
- certainty
- compassion
- integrity
- intelligence
- success
- significance
- growth
- education
- happiness
- contribution

In life we tend to admire people who take a stand for what they believe in, and we are in awe of those extraordinary people who live by highly defined principles. Consider Nelson Mandela. He spent three decades in prison, and upon his release his convictions towards human rights were as strong as when he was jailed. Martin Luther King, Jr., lived a life congruently by his values in his role as a prominent leader in the African American civil rights movement. Mother Teresa lived her life through love, connection, and contribution. For more than forty-five years she ministered to the poor, sick, orphaned, and dying, while she guided the Missionaries of Charity's expansion first throughout India and then in other countries. Think of anyone you have admired in your life and notice how strongly they stand by their values and how clear they were on their direction.

Often we subordinate ourselves to outside influences and get caught up living a life based on our perceived ideas of what it is we should be focusing on. For example, I worked with a client who was experiencing challenges around comparison. She found herself constantly comparing her life to that of her friends. She reflected on their marriages and their children, the clothes they brought, and the amount of friends they had. The list went on, and the conversation went something like this: "I feel like I should be getting married, having children, and moving to the suburbs. I'm so far behind and it stresses me out." As we explored this challenge and reflected on her long-term relationship with her man, I worked with her to begin to understand the different values at play. We reflected on the comparisons as a simple example of getting the results in life that you value most. Her friends valued marriage and family much more highly than topics such as wealth creation, career progression, travel, and adventure. This is why they lived happily in the suburbs with a family of five. Their decisions in life had moved them to this space. At the heart of it all, my client didn't really want these results. She just thought she did based on a conditioning that it was the "right thing to do"—someone else's values imposed on her during her upbringing.

When you set goals or push yourself in the direction of goals that are not in alignment with your true values, then you set yourself up for failure. You become critical of yourself and are essentially betraying what it is you truly desire to achieve. In the space of your true and highest values, discipline, order, reliability, focus, and mastery will come naturally. However, in the space of those values that are lowest on your list, chaos, frustration, critique of self, and a sense of hardship will prevail. When my client was pushing to create a life in alignment to the results of her friends, she was going against the grain of her own values, resulting in an endless struggle characterised by comparison and a tiring sense of self-betrayal. Until she was able to connect with what it was *she* truly wanted to achieve, the void was being filled with her perceived sense of fulfillment and self-worth based on the lives of others. Neither value set is right or wrong, and this is simply an example of each individual seeking to fill a void that gives meaning and fulfillment to life. When you are not aware of the values you are seeking to attain, then you cannot move to achieve a satisfying life. The paradox here is that you already know what it is you don't know. You just haven't stopped to acknowledge it yet.

Defining Your Values

What are your top five values, and are you living a life congruent to what you value most? When I first ask clients this question, I am frequently greeted by a blank stare. Their eyes rattle furiously as they attempt to access what they value most because it sounds like a simple enough question, yet when it comes to answering it, many people have no idea where to start. It's a simple yet powerful question, one which requires you to probe deeper into your possibilities, including who you are and what makes you shine. And the probing reveals fascinating insights. I heard human behaviour specialist, speaker, and author Dr. John Demartini explain at a conference once how your biggest void growing up as a child will drive your current focus. There is a yearning inside you to find the hidden order in life. You want to know the answers to the questions where you perceive the biggest void. Whatever is most missing or most misunderstood becomes valuable, and values fill your voids. Whatever you think is most missing you will seek to achieve.

The things you hold highest or describe as most important begin to provide insights to your values. To determine your own values, you can begin by making a list of all those emotions or qualities that have meaning and heart for you. A full exercise titled "Defining Your Values" is further outlined in the "Exercises for Reflection" section at the end of this chapter. While an initial list of emotions and qualities that you hold high are an important place to start, you can then also reflect on five key areas.

1. **Passion**

   Passion as a strong affection or enthusiasm can be harnessed to determine those areas in life where you allow your true self to shine.

2. **Organisation**

   The areas in your life where you are most organised provide clues on your highest values. This refers to the tasks, topics, or themes where nobody has to motivate you to get organised.

3. **Money as energy**

   In her work *The Energy of Money*, Maria Nemeth quotes, "How you do money is how you do life. Our relationship with money is a metaphor for our relationship with all forms of energy: time, physical vitality, enjoyment, creativity and the support of friends."

   With this in mind, the reflection on your relationship with money is a key insight in terms of defining your values.

4. **Time in the diary**

   Time is an interesting concept, as you cannot get your time back, making it an incredibly valuable asset. How you choose to use it also provides powerful insights as to what you perceive is most important.

5. An attitude of gratitude

Imagination is a glimpse in to the future, and what you have most focused on and thought about will now be coming to fruition. The parts of this manifestation that you choose to show gratitude for reflect the areas of most importance and provide a valuable insight into your core values.

When you work to define your values it is also important to reflect on your hierarchy of order in terms of what values you hold highest. You have a hierarchy of values where you value one thing over the other, starting with your top value, going to your next most essential value, and then moving down the hierarchy. It is this order of priority that dictates your destiny because your decisions will be influenced based on your defined hierarchy.

To achieve fulfillment and true success in life, it is essential to know what you value most and then commit to living by these values each and every day. Your values must hold true not just when the going is easy, but when the going is tough as well.

Writing Your Guidebook

Once you have defined your top five values, it is important that you get clear on creating a life in alignment to the things that bring you the most happiness. Your guidebook determines what must happen in order for you to meet your values and to feel happiness and fulfillment. For example, one of my values is health and vitality, and I have specific guidelines to ensure I meet this value. I am experiencing health and vitality when I am doing the following:

- eating foods as close to their original source as possible, including limiting all processed foods and choosing organic and free range options;
- eating fruit and vegetables daily—at least two to five pieces;
- drinking lots of water and green juice;
- allowing time for self-care and meditation;
- practicing yoga at least twice per week; and
- exercising three times per week or more (walking, yoga, or cycling).

Like a fingerprint, each set of values is unique because they are supported by your own personal guidelines. Each person with health and vitality on their values list will have a different interpretation as to what this value means to them. They will also then have unique guidelines that drive the way in which they determine how to meet this value, and they will awaken to anything that supports meeting their value while they shy away from those things that do not.

❧

**Your guidebook determines what must happen
in order for you to experience fulfillment.**

❧

One important area to note when you are setting your guidelines is the level of challenge you set for yourself. For the value of health and vitality, a guideline that states, "I must exercise every day," or, "I must be continuing to lose weight always," is a recipe for self-sabotage, as both of these commitments are intense and not sustainable. For example, you cannot continue to lose weight every day, or you will simply fade away to nothingness. The commitment to exercise every day is equally as challenging, as on some days this may not be physically possible—for example, if you become unwell and need to rest. Setting up guidelines that are unattainable or incredibly challenging to achieve creates roadblocks to your own access to happiness. For some people the creation of difficult guidelines is a strategy that puts success and achievement out of reach, reinforcing an underlying belief around not being worthy of love or happiness. With this in mind, as you create your guidelines for each of your values, remember to make

53

sure your guides are realistic and give yourself space to meet your values in a variety of ways. When you are clear on what it is you value the most and how you choose to meet those values, then essentially you have mapped out the specific things that lead to contentment, as you define it. This is your happiness recipe.

Bringing Values Together in Love

Many clients often ask me, "Is it possible for a relationship to function when the fundamental values of each individual are so different?" Often coaching sessions centre on the challenge of dealing with different value sets within a relationship context because people link the need for sameness to relationship success. Yet at the core of this issue is the frame of focus through which the original question is posed. The question presupposes that different value sets and dysfunction are linked. People often feel stuck when it comes to value differences, and at the heart of this quality of being stuck is the perception that the differences need fixing. Yet it's not the values that need to shift to a place of sameness but rather the perception and appreciation associated with celebrating the differences. The celebration of differences will be a common theme throughout this book. I truly do believe that it is the celebration of differences that reframes and reshapes many of the relationship challenges we are experiencing in society today.

I heard author and human potential coach Dr. John Demartini describe an ideal definition of love at a seminar I once attended. His definition was based on an ancient Greek definition that says, "If you have too many similarities without differences, then you have infatuation. If you have too many differences without similarities, then you have resentment. If you have a perfect balance of similarities and differences, then you have love."

This is why in a relationship you are going to find you have both support and challenge. Your partner can be nice and then mean. They can be kind and then cruel. They give and then take. They can lift you up when you're feeling down and then quickly bring you back down to earth when you are getting too ahead of yourself. Demartini explains that if you expect all of the positive aspects without the balance, then you have an unrealistic expectation on human behaviour. The same applies when one is acknowledging values. Anytime you expect another individual to live outside of their values, you are going to be betrayed. Demartini so accurately states, "Betrayal is never what somebody does to you; betrayal is what *you* do to you by projecting your values on to somebody else and then by expecting them to be making decisions according to your values and not their own."

To take this one step further, notice how attentive and creative you are in the areas that are highest on your value list, and on the opposing side, acknowledge the balance and level of destruction you create in the areas that are lowest on your value list. With this frame of reference, you might also notice the value of attracting someone into your life who works to complement your areas of creativity and destruction. Whatever you try to disown in yourself, you keep attracting to yourself. For example, if there is someone in your life who drives you up the wall with his or her rigid routine or structured approach to life and if you choose to have little or nothing to do with that person, you will then soon meet another person who you will come to realise has the same traits. You are surrounded by people who represent your disowned parts. You can't escape them. Instead you must choose to learn from them and to build a relationship to love those parts of yourself.

The secret is to honor your partner and know that he or she is going to make decisions according to his or her values and not yours. Avoid the urge to create a sense of sameness and instead celebrate the differences and the unique hierarchy of values for each individual. Like a fingerprint, for every single person in the world there is a unique value set based on the guidelines we assign and the meanings we give things. For every unique value set there is then someone else in the world who will have the complete opposite values. This creates a beautiful harmony of reflection in our world where there is no right or wrong, no good or bad, simply what is true for each individual.

**By celebrating differences we reshape many of
the relationship challenges in society today.**

When you can truly embrace this concept of acceptance, then
your candle can shine brightly to support the atmosphere for *Love
on the Kitchen Table*. Once individual values are defined, the next
step is to take these as the foundation and work together to define
the values for your relationship based on your combined list of
individual traits. Some questions for consideration are included
at the end of this chapter in the "Exercises for Reflection" section.
When you reach this point, enjoy working through the questions
together with your partner.

Chapter Summary

Getting clear on your own values helps you to recognise what
is important to you so you can truly know yourself, make effective
decisions, and live your life to its full potential. As part of living
to your potential, you must find ways to meet your values every
day—not some of your values but all of them. When we live lives
closely aligned to our values, we can experience happiness more
often. The combination of two strong individuals who know their
values then represents an incredible bond, one similar to the glow
of two strong candles that set the mood for the magic to follow.

Exercises for Reflection

Section 1: Your Recipe to Happiness: Defining Your Values

Follow the steps below to determine your top five values. You can refer back to the additional details in the chapter as needed. Complete the first part of the exercise—steps 1, 2, and 3—on your own and then share your responses with your partner as part of the second section to define your relationship values.

Step 1: Defining Your Values

Begin by brainstorming ten or more key states, emotions, or qualities that you highly value.

1. _____

2. _____

3. _____

4. _____

5. _____

6. _____

7. _____

8. _____

9. _____

10 _____

Next work through the following five areas to add to your list:

1. **Passion**

   Passion as a strong affection or enthusiasm can be harnessed to determine those areas in life where you allow your true self to shine. What is it that gets your juices flowing? What are the specific topics that you could talk all day and night about? What are the topics that have you incredibly curious and eager to know more? List five or more areas in your life you are passionate about.

2. **Organisation**

   Reflect on where in your life you are most organised. This refers to the tasks, topics, or themes where nobody has to motivate you to get organised. You simply tend to have these areas of your life under control in an easy and effortless flow. List five or more areas in your life where you are most organised.

3. **Money as energy**

   In her work *The Energy of Money*, Maria Nemeth quotes, "How you do money is how you do life. Our relationship with money is a metaphor for our relationship with all forms of energy: time, physical vitality, enjoyment, creativity and the support of friends."

With this in mind, the reflection on your relationship with money is a key insight in terms of defining your values. List five or more areas in your life where you most commonly direct your money energy.

4. **Time in the diary**

Time is an interesting concept, as you cannot get your time back, making it an incredibly valuable asset. How you choose to use it also provides powerful insights as to what you perceive is most important. When you reflect on your weekly diary or timetable, what is it that fills your time? Once you have brainstormed these major blocks of activity, next reflect on how you would spend an ideal day outside of the space of your daily routine. List five or more areas in your life where you choose to spend your time.

5. **An attitude of gratitude**

What are you most grateful for in your life right now? Imagination is a glimpse in to the future, and what you have most focused on and thought about will now be coming to fruition. The parts of this manifestation that you choose to show gratitude for reflect the areas of most importance and provide a valuable insight into your core values. List five or more areas of your life that you are most grateful for right now.

Step 2: Setting Your Hierarchy

Review your list of values and begin to group each of the items into five common themes. To reduce your list, look for items that are similar to others. For example, growth, education, books, and learning might be grouped under one value—knowledge. Remember, dropping or combining values from your list doesn't mean that you no longer value them. Rather, the exercise of reduction helps more clearly define your top priorities. Once you are down to your top five values, list them in order of importance. To check the order, ask yourself, "If I had to choose to give up either value one or value two, which one would I choose to give up?" Work your way through your list to define the hierarchy of your top five values.

1. _____

2. _____

3. _____

4. _____

5. _____

- What is it you have learnt from doing this exercise?

- Were you surprised by the order of your top five values?

- Do you feel you are living your life congruently with these values?

- Are any of your values conflicting? For example, do you value security *and* freedom? If so, how do these fit together?

Step 3: Exploring Your Guidelines

Take the time now to write down the guidelines for your top five values. Remember to focus on creating as many resourceful and varied ways of living by your values as possible to increase your access to happiness.

Value 1

Guidelines

_____

_____

_____

_____

_____

Value 2

Guidelines

_____

_____

_____

_____

_____

Value3

Guidelines

_____

_____

_____

_____

Value 4

Guidelines

_____

_____

_____

_____

_____

Value 5

Guidelines

_____

_____

_____

_____

_____

_____

_____

Section 2: Defining Relationship Values

Now that you have worked through the first part of the exercise on your own, it's time to share your thoughts and feelings with your loved one. Spend some time sharing the results of your individual value work and then work through the following questions to determine your joint relationship values as guided by your individual ones.

- When you review both your value lists side by side, what do you notice is unique about the combination of values and guidelines specific to your relationship?

- What makes your relationship so magical?

- How would other people (friends and family) describe your relationship?

- What are the top five values of your relationship?

- What is it you stand for as a united couple?

- What is the five-year, ten-year, twenty-year, and lifetime vision for your relationship?

Chapter 3

The Essential Tools: The Ten Core Needs of an Ideal Relationship

The expectations of life depend upon diligence;
the mechanic that would perfect his
work must first sharpen his tools.

—Confucius

A Native American grandfather was talking to his grandson about how he felt. He explained how he often envisioned two wolves fighting in his heart. He described the feeling of the tension and pull of conflict. "One wolf is incredibly vengeful, full of anger and violence, while the other wolf is loving and compassionate," he explained.

Curious, the grandson asked his grandfather, "Which of the wolves will win the fight of your heart?"

The grandfather smiled and answered based on years of wisdom. "The one I feed," he said.

All possibilities exist within you, yet it is the possibilities you choose to feed or what you choose to focus on that will determine the results you get in life. If you feed the wolf of hardship, then you will experience hardship. If you feed the wolf of financial pressure, then you will experience financial pressure. Instead you must feed the wolf that best serves you to achieve your dreams and desires—in this case, the relationship results you would most like to experience. So far as part of the *Love on the Kitchen Table* model, we've built a solid foundation of beliefs and lit the candles for each of the value sets to shine. Next it's time to explore the tools we need to eat our food. Just as we need to decide what to set the table with to nurture and support our meal—knives and forks, salt and pepper, salad dressing—we must also decide on the tools we need to create lasting love, growth, and fulfillment.

**The possibilities you choose to focus
on will determine your results.**

The relationship model explored in this chapter highlights the ten core needs necessary to make up an ideal relationship. In the words of Canadian philosopher Marshall McLuhan, "We become what we behold. We shape our tools and then our tools shape us."

The Relationship Plate of Core Needs

The relationship plate of core needs has been developed to demonstrate the essential elements that make up a successful relationship. The model is composed of two key levels: (1) the six core needs of individual human behaviour and (2) the four core needs of the ideal relationship. It is important to understand that before you begin a journey of having a relationship with your significant other, you must first have a relationship with yourself. When you can acknowledge that you are whole and complete within yourself, then you can experience an intimate relationship with another human being on a more complete and spiritual level. In comparison, a relationship based on the need for completion can be codependent and detrimental, where individuals are fixated on the needs of or control of another. This later state involves placing a lower priority on one's own needs while being excessively preoccupied with the needs of others. We'll discuss this further throughout the chapter; however, for now it is essential to understand that a relationship with self must precede a successful intimate relationship.

In the *relationship plate of core needs* model, the ideal relationship rests at the core of the model. The six core needs of individual human behaviour then detail the first level of focus as the initial building blocks of success. These core needs are (1) certainty, (2) variety, (3) significance, (4) love and connection, (5) growth, and (6) contribution. The next layer of the model details four core relationship needs. These are (1) friendship, (2) love, (3) creation, and (4) identity.

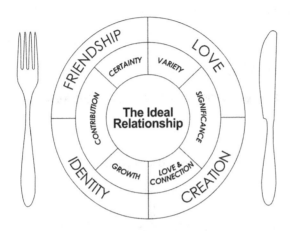

Each of these core needs exists to protect and nurture the ideal relationship in the centre of the plate to keep the connection strong, alive, fulfilling, and driven by purpose. Knowledge is power, and when you are clear on where to direct your focus, then the desired states become more easily attainable. The relationship plate of core needs provides a structure based on experience and success, detailing where to direct your focus on both an individual and a relationship level. As you read about each of the key elements that make up an ideal connection, you may already begin to recognise the ways in which you do or do not embrace these ideals. As you begin to notice the gaps in your own world, be assured that you are already making the changes necessary to fill the voids with more resourceful thinking, actions, and results. The true gift of this chapter is the awareness of a model of thinking that can guide you to focus on key areas of influence. You then choose which wolf to feed.

Individual Needs:
The Six Core Needs of Human Behaviour

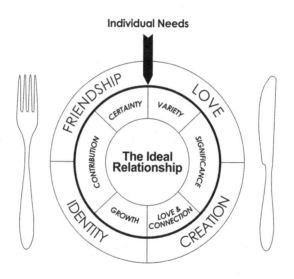

At the core of our relationships rests two individual personalities, each with their own set of needs. While the relationship as a whole has certain needs that must be met, on an individual level we also have specific needs. When you can understand these individual and relationship needs in the context of each other, then you have a magnified understanding for the structure of the core elements that make up a successful relationship. The art of fulfillment is then the ability to tap into the core needs that drive decision making to better shape your results, levels of satisfaction, and ability to contribute.

The concept that we all live our lives to meet six core needs is based on the work done by leading coach and inspirational speaker Anthony Robbins. Through his work with millions of people around the world, he concludes that six core needs drive human behaviour and serve as the basis of every choice we make. These core needs are (1) certainty, (2) variety, (3) significance, (4) love and connection, (5) growth, and (6) contribution. Anthony Robbins claims that every decision and every direction we choose is based on our innate need to satisfy this selection of needs.

The majority of people don't even know these needs exist. As simple as it sounds, few people know what they most want in life, and even fewer consistently focus on getting it. Instead most people focus on the means to getting what they want rather than the core need that is driving the action itself. For example, people obsess over ideals such as *success* or *money*, yet these are simply the means for meeting their core needs—in this case, likely *significance* and *certainty*.

The six core needs can be broken down into two categories. The first four needs are known as the needs of the personality, and they include the following: (1) certainty, (2) variety, (3) significance, and (4) love and connection.

The final two core needs are then the needs of the spirit, and they include (5) growth and (6) contribution.

The six core needs of human behaviour are not merely wants or desires, but rather they are innate needs that you strive always to achieve. You may achieve your needs in resourceful, neutral, and unresourceful ways, where the unresourceful strategies are often your sticking points that create conflict and unhappiness. We will explore these strategies further in this chapter, yet for now it's essential to know that your goal in self-improvement is to focus on positive ways to meet each of your core needs to create a harmonious flow of energy and contentment. When you can zoom out and reflect on each of these core needs as the drivers of human behavior, then you can begin to better understand the impact they have on your own life.

A deeper look at each of the core needs follows, including my own interpretation and examples of how each of the individual needs can be met both resourcefully and unresourcefully in an individual and relationship context. As you explore each of the concepts, you will begin to notice the ways in which you currently meet these needs within your own life, including the association and impact on your relationship. The key is this: The more resourceful ways you have to meet each of the core needs, the more access to happiness and satisfaction you will create within your world.

Certainty (Security and Comfort)

Certainty refers to your innate need for security and stability. This need is about achieving order and control in your life to give you a template of assurance that allows you to understand what comes next. Certainty is displayed most commonly through feeling safe and having a comfortable physical environment. On an individual level resourceful examples of meeting a need for certainty might include the establishment of a consistent routine, one that creates a supportive environment that nurtures the goals you are working to achieve. Creating a safe, warm home with a kitchen full of fresh foods and entertainment to keep you stimulated is an example of a system of comfort and certainty that grounds you to your sense of self. In addition to these external examples of certainty, having strong self-confidence and trust in self is an internal example of how the core need of certainty can be achieved.

Unresourceful displays of certainty on an individual level might include fostering the unhealthy need to control others. This type of behaviour is incredibly unresourceful, as the only real thing you can control is your own reaction to the events around you, not the events or the behaviour of others. The specific elements that make up your routine and system for living can also be very unresourceful, particularly where they are adopted as part of an avoidance or low self-esteem strategy. For example, watching excessive amounts of TV, playing interactive games for hours on end, and overeating comfort foods are all examples of strategies that can be unresourceful, particularly when used to avoid interacting with everyday life. These types of activities are substituted for the activity that is being avoided and act as replacement pillars of certainty. Low self-esteem or lack of certainty within self can also result in actions such as staying in a relationship or career when you are not happy. Once again this type of behaviour often takes place to support an innate need for certainty, so while you may not be truly happy, you hold on to the pillars of comfort.

In a relationship context the more times your partner comes through to support you, the more you will begin to build on your level of certainty and trust. Moving through each of the stages of intimacy can create resourceful certainty and stability within love. As a broad overview, the "I love you" stage through to the "moving in together" and the "long-term commitment of marriage" stage are examples of relationship milestones that build upon each other to create a sense of stability, comfort, and certainty.

Unresourceful strategies for meeting the core need of certainty in a relationship context might include the need to control your partner, including where he or she goes, what he or she wears, what he or she says, and with whom he or she interacts with. This type of behaviour is often linked to a lack of trust in self and low self-esteem, where a substitute manipulative physical need for certainty is sought instead. The result is a relationship halted by such stringent controls that growth and contribution are unable to take place.

Variety (Challenges and Adventure)

The second core need is variety, which works in tension with the need for certainty. If life is saturated with too much certainty, then you will experience boredom and find yourself craving variety and adventure. In the same way, if life is too chaotic, you will find yourself craving simplicity and comfort. Like a beautifully swinging pendulum, the challenge is to satisfy both needs resourcefully. You create a level of chaos that you then work to make sense of, bringing it back to certainty. Once you have made sense of the chaos and achieved certainty, you then create your next challenge. In a content state you are constantly learning and vibrating at new levels, swinging between the stability of certainty and the challenge of variety. As part of this balance, variety is the state that encourages experiencing new and novel activities, which can meet physical, emotional, mental, or spiritual needs. A reflective question to ask yourself to explore your own levels of variety is this: When was the last time you did something for the first time? Variety is about learning new things, exploring new hobbies, and challenging yourself with increased levels of creativity. As opposed to the grounding sensation of certainty, variety involves great movement and pushing through the boundary conditions of your comfort zone.

Aleisha Coote

Contentment is swinging between the stability of certainty and the challenge of variety.

Unresourceful ways of meeting a need for variety might include the creation of a schedule so full of activities that you become disconnected with life itself. This can often lead to a strategy of being stressed or a breakdown that ironically ensures you then begin to experience a level of groundedness and certainty. Of a similar nature, the bright shiny syndrome is another form of self-sabotage driven by a need for variety, where you constantly start a range of new activities yet never commit to consistency or completion. The excessive consumption of alcohol and other drugs are examples of unresourceful strategies for creating variety and adventure. These examples lead to self-sabotage and destruction.

Within a relationship context, resourceful variety is extremely important and keeps the relationship growing. Pick a new restaurant to explore, take cooking classes together, or book a romantic getaway to an exotic location that neither of you has ever visited before. The key is to approach new activities with a childlike sense of fun. Open yourself up to the vulnerability of learning something new or the adventure of exploring the unknown. The best part is that you have a partner to share the experience with. When variety in a relationship is achieved on a consistent level, the relationship is kept alive, refreshing, and satisfying for both parties.

One of the most unresourceful ways to seek variety in a relationship is through the creation of drama. Picking fights to simply have something to do is a common way to achieve variety for some people. On an unconscious level you create a shake-up within the relationship to break free from the boredom of certainty. Yet this strategy simply brings about drama, conflict, and grievances. The majority of people stay focused on the drama and never really understand the core need they are striving to achieve, most likely variety. If you recognise this in your own world, please know that often what you are really looking for is more variety or something new to do. Once you can acknowledge the core need driving your behaviour, then you can begin to look for more resourceful ways to create variety, adventure, or action.

Significance (Important, Special, and Unique)

Significance is the third core need and refers to the innate desire to feel important, special, and unique. On an individual level, significance can be achieved by a range of activities, specifically being a leader of self and of others. Leading by example and having others follow your lead can have a remarkable ripple effect, prompting emotions associated with achievement, pride, and a feeling of worthiness. The achievement of goals and mastery in a certain field can also prompt feelings of significance based on what you believe success and achievement mean to you. Sponsoring a child in an underprivileged community or committing to charity and volunteer work are other resourceful ways to experience significance and a feeling of being needed.

As with all the core needs, significance can also be gained through unresourceful means. Examples include the shifting of energy in the form of putting others down, interrogation, and bullying for your own self-gain. Connecting to a destructive identity or behaviour pattern, such as being a martyr, victim, or rebel, are additional forms of seeking significance. Drug circles and gang members also fall under this category, where being part of the group feeds a need for significance at the expense of others.

Significance as a core need has an interesting impact on relationships. As with the first two core needs (certainty and variety), significance works in tension with the fourth core need— love and connection. The same rule applies. If you immerse yourself too much in gaining personal significance, then you will have trouble keeping strong relationships that thrive on love and connection. If you are too focused on the "what's in it for me" element of life, then you will never truly be able to open your heart to give to others. In the same sense, if you immerse yourself too deeply in love and connection, giving all of yourself to others in an unresourcefully selfless manner, then you can lose touch with your own sense of identity and the significance associated with being comfortable in your own skin. The tension between significance and love and connection is a balance that needs to be achieved in a harmonious manner.

Love and Connection (Approval and Attachment)

Love and connection is the fourth core need and relates to the need to experience connection and attachment to other human beings. Man was not created to exist in isolation, and the success or the lack of success in your most intimate relationships will have a direct impact on your overall happiness and fulfillment in life. It is therefore essential to surround yourself with supportive, nurturing relationships that allow you to grow as a unique individual. Love must be considered as a verb, where you work to achieve success in this area and invest in your relationship—just as you would in spring cleaning your home or servicing your car. If you want more love, you must do it more often.

Love and connection is such an innate human need that people will seek connection in any form available. Destructive forms of connection might include emotionally abusive behaviour or physical violence, where connection is achieved through force and manipulation is undertaken. At the more submissive end of the scale, unhealthy relationships can also be based on emotionally needy circumstances or victimhood, where people can become rescuers in order to meet their need for love and connection. Again the focus is on the means to achieving this need, and the question to ask is this: "Am I meeting my need for love and connection in a resourceful way?" The challenge is that people are not even aware of the need they are striving to meet. Therefore, the behaviours are viewed out of context until we can put them into basic perspective and begin to search for more resourceful strategies and outcomes to meet our needs.

Anthony Robbins refers to these first four needs as the needs of the personality, where the key needs that drive your behaviour and your way of meeting these needs define your unique personality. These needs of the personality are physical needs that you will endeavor to meet no matter what. If you are unable to meet these needs resourcefully, then you will revert to unresourceful methods. This all happens on an unconscious level. For example, you may not be aware that you are manifesting illness or another state that requires care and attention in order to meet your need for love and connection. Or perhaps you are creating drama in your life as a means to achieving variety.

The final two core needs are then known as the needs of the spirit, where true fulfillment is reached by mastering resourceful ways to meet the needs of growth and contribution. The meaning you give your life and the meaning you crave come from your ability to resourcefully meet these final two needs.

Growth (Progress and Development)

Growth refers to the need for constant emotional, intellectual, and spiritual development. This type of development is required to make you feel alive and to demonstrate you are progressing in life and learning new things. Because when life becomes too predictable, you become restless and eager to discover your next challenge. In his book *The Celestine Prophecy*, author James Redfield describes growth as a lifetime journey of mastering how to live. He says, "Every human being, whether conscious of it or not, illustrates with their lives how he or she thinks a human being is supposed to live." He talks about improving on the paths of your ancestors, specifically the parents you were born to. He writes,

> We are not merely the physical creation of our parents; we are also the spiritual creation. You were born to these two people and their lives had an irrevocable effect on who you are. To discover your real self, you must admit that the real you began in a position between their truths. That's why you were born there: to take a higher perspective on what they stood for. Your path is about discovering a truth that is a higher synthesis of what these two people believed.

This is one way to view growth, progress, and development as a core human need.

In a most basic form, if you're not growing, then you're dying. You must be moving forward and developing yourself in some way, and the level at which you commit to meeting your need for growth will directly coincide with your level of happiness and fulfillment. Often you get caught up in the day-to-day routine of life. Yet when you stop to reflect on all the ways in which you are progressing and developing, then you can really begin to appreciate the fulfillment that comes from meeting this core need. These are three key questions to ask yourself on a daily basis:

How did I grow today?

What new things did I learn?

How did I improve myself emotionally, intellectually, and spiritually?

When two motivated individuals respect their emotional, intellectual, and spiritual development and then come together to combine forces, a profound energy is created. Growth is essential to living a fulfilling life, and Anthony Robbins so appropriately reminds us that "the only true security in life comes from knowing that every single day you are improving yourself in some way."

Contribution (Service to Others)

The final individual core need is about contribution beyond the self, where the secret to living is giving. This core need is about embracing life as a gift that offers you the privilege, opportunity, and responsibility to give back to the world by becoming something more than just a participating member of society. Anthony Robbins says, "It's not what we get, but who we become and what we contribute that gives true meaning to our lives." The ultimate question to ask yourself is this: "How can I serve others with that which exists within me right now?" The act of contribution has the power to change lives. Helping someone else in need changes the dynamics for everyone involved and can create a ripple effect of change beyond the limits of your current thinking.

Embrace contribution beyond the self.
Ask yourself, "How can I serve others
with that which exists within me?"

Whether you choose to give monetary donations, give blood, donate physical items, or offer your time or services to benefit the lives of others, your contribution makes a difference and serves to make the world a better place.

As an individual, you strive to meet each of these six core needs always, yet you also have a dominant two or three needs that you will seek to meet more often. These dominant needs will form your lead system and will tilt the direction of your decisions and the consequent results you get in life. As a generalistation, people with higher levels of masculinity tend to need more significance, variety, and growth, while those with higher levels of feminine energy tend to need more certainty, connection, and contribution. This is interesting to note in the context of your relationship and helps to make sense of the core needs that may be driving your loved one's behaviour. The key is to recognise what need you are seeking to meet at any one time because this then determines how you go about each aspect of your life and the decisions you are making. For example, if an event happens that triggers limiting emotions, such as anger, frustration, or sadness, you must acknowledge that what has really happened is that a certain need has become challenged or threatened. When you begin to acknowledge this frame of thinking, you can then begin to tweak your reactions to events so that you can instead focus on a proactive and more resourceful way to have your identified need met rather than living in a state of reaction.

There are three ways to meet your six core individual needs: (1) through unresourceful, low-quality vehicles, (2) through neutral vehicles, and (3) through resourceful, high-quality vehicles. For example, unresourceful ways to meet the core need of variety might include taking drugs and drinking excessive alcohol, indulging in destructive activities or self-sabotage, or creating a negative drama cycle within your everyday world. Neutral vehicles for meeting this same need might include smaller-scale examples of creating variety—for example, ensuring you have different breakfast choices, creating variety in your daily outfits, or choosing to go to bed at a different time each night. While these neutral vehicles might not seem to have a significant impact, in their small form they still illustrate the opportunity for choice. In comparison more resourceful, high-quality vehicles for achieving variety might include embracing travel adventures, creating new challenges, learning new hobbies, and encouraging creativity. Think of your core needs like a petrol barrel that gets filled with the goodness of satisfaction. Unresourceful, low-quality vehicles deplete the barrel of all goodness. Neutral vehicles put goodness into the barrel yet at a very small rate so that further input is still required. Of greatest impact are the high-quality vehicles that fill the barrel with a high amount of goodness and satisfaction. Taking a holiday to a new location or choosing to do renovations on your home may be more substantial vehicles for meeting your need of variety.

Individual Needs and Your Relationship

Your intimate relationship with your significant other is one vehicle for meeting your core needs, yet it must not be the *only* vehicle. Instead what's important to note is the level at which your relationship with another individual meets all of your six core needs because this defines the intimacy experienced. For example, a relationship that satisfies two of the six core needs can be defined as a connection. A relationship that satisfies four of the six core needs can be defined as a bond, and a relationship that satisfies all six core needs can be defined as intimate—one you will not want to give up! As mentioned, your relationship must not be your only way to meet your individual core needs. Rather, it is just one element. Along these lines, the ultimate goal is to establish many resourceful, high-quality vehicles to meet each of your six core needs. The emphasis on having various different vehicles for meeting your core needs is key because if you only have one vehicle and it is taken away from you, then you will experience great pain. An example of this is getting caught up in a full-time focus on a specific job or project. If your only focus is the project over a sustained period of time and then the project falls through or ends, then you will be left with a massive gap in terms of meeting your core needs. Professional athletes often experience this gap after the completion of a major event or competition where they've trained for a long period of time, often years, and they are then left with the feeling of having no purpose following the completion of the sporting event or milestone they were striving to achieve. What must happen is new resourceful vehicles must quickly be sought to fill the gap and regain satisfaction. The more resourceful, sustainable vehicles you have, the better.

The layers represented in the relationship plate of core needs are of significant importance in that both the personal needs must be met in order to then support the relationship needs. A prevalent issue in society is the concept of thinking that when we meet our significant others, they "complete us." The issue with this level of thinking is that it presupposes we were broken in the first place. Rather, you must strive for completeness and wholeness within yourself, which will then exist within the realm of your relationship. When two whole individuals come together in romantic love, a divine power is created, and the relationship exists at a much higher level. The key difference is that the individuals are not pulled off their own paths of evolution and instead remain strong in themselves *and* as part of the relationship.

You must strive for wholeness within
yourself, which will then exist within
the realm of your relationship.

What this means is that the six core needs of human behaviour must be met on an individual level, where the relationship may be viewed as *one* of the high-quality vehicles to achieving your needs. However, it is not seen as the only vehicle, and it is definitely not the part that makes you complete. You are already whole and complete, and you should meet the six core needs of human behaviour based on your own unique identity. This is why these human-based needs form the inner circle surrounding the ideal relationship. Once these needs can be fully met on an individual level, then the focus of the relationship elements are magnified to a more powerful, sustainable flow. The joining of two complete individuals leads to something new and much greater than each alone could generate.

Relationship Needs:
The Four Core Needs of an Ideal Relationship

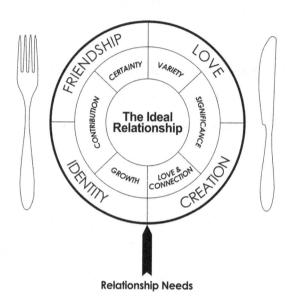

Relationship Needs

Now that you have explored the first layer of individual core needs, you have a solid understanding of the core needs that you and your loved one must first seek to fulfill on an individual level. Next the second layer of the relationship plate of core needs details the four essential elements required to sustain an ideal relationship. The elements detailed in this part of the model are concepts that I have further developed based on the work of relationship coach, trainer, and much-loved mentor Alice Haemmerle. As part of her extensive coaching work with couples around the world, Alice

Haemmerle proposed three key components that she believes make up a fulfilling and lasting connection, three componets universal to all ideal relationships. The role of (1) lovers, (2) best friends, and (3) creators are detailed in Alice Haemmerle's original model, and I have continued to develop this level of thinking to also include (4) relationship identity and mission. Each of these four components exists to protect and nurture the ideal relationship in the centre of the plate and to keep the connection strong, alive, fulfilling, and driven by a common purpose. When one of the components breaks down or becomes neglected, frustration and unhappiness are inevitable. This is one of the key reasons many relationships collapse—the focus of the connection fails to encompass one or more of the relationship's core needs. This next section of the chapter looks at each of these relationship core needs in more depth, beginning with friendship.

Friendship (Best Friends and Strength)

Many relationships begin in the space of friendship where a connection is created and then blossoms into love and intimacy. Friendships are based on a bond of similarities and a foundation of trust, where each party in a friendship brings a unique element to the partnership, and when the two are combined, they are stronger as a whole. This combined force means the core need of friendship provides strength for the ideal relationship. Strength and trust then supports a balance of emotional polarity. The best friend element in your partner picks you up when you're feeling down, and then at the other end of the continuum, it levels you out when your thinking becomes ego-driven. The ability to provide support at both ends of the continuum allows the relationship to ride through both the good and bad times based on a continuous stream of support.

Best friends talk for hours on end, share their most intimate thoughts, and are always there to help each other out. Best friends play, explore, laugh, and joke together, taking a light-hearted approach to life that is based on a solid foundation of trust. The strength of this core need keeps the relationship growing and full of variety. You can tell your best friend anything and feel confident that you won't be judged. You give your best friend flexibility when it comes to life and often bend over backwards to help them out when they need it. When you've got your best friend in your life, anything is possible. This core need is essential in creating the ideal relationship.

Love (Lovers and Passion)

It is important to understand that love as an overarching theme surrounds all of the needs in the relationship plate of core needs. What this particular element is referring to is the concept of love in a passionate sense. It refers to the role of lovers, where being with your lover is not in the context of family, friends, and children but rather in the sense of a passionate state of intimacy. This element relates to sex, romance, and the incredible animalistic attraction that exists within passion. Full of energy and fire, the concept of *opposites attracting* is key in understanding the power that fuels this passion. Opposing sexual energy is explored further in chapter 9; however, as a brief snapshot, sexual polarity can be described as the force of passion that arcs between the masculine and feminine poles. It is here where opposites really do attract and where the attractive difference between the masculine and feminine energies becomes the key for ongoing passion. This passion can be described as the fiery life of the relationship, and it is what sets the relationship apart from other relationships, such as those with friends, colleagues, and other family members.

The friendship and love elements from the relationship plate of core needs are often very strong in the beginning of a relationship. In fact, the majority of people begin their relationships as best friends and then become lovers, or they are lovers who then become best friends. These two components are vital for an ideal relationship, and when they exist at a high level, naturally they progress to the next core need, where one plus one equals three.

Creation (Parents and Fulfillment)

The third component of an ideal relationship involves giving birth to something outside of the relationship. This element doesn't necessarily refer to giving birth to a child. Rather, it can be anything where you and your lover come together to invest time and focus in something external. It may be the birthing of a business, holiday plans, a new pet, or the growth of a family garden. It may be moving in together and creating a new home that is uniquely yours, which you then cherish and look after. The key characteristics of this element are love, growth, and nurturance. Love in the form of desire is required to want to move towards the creation and investment in the external. Commitment to growth then represents the power that drives the energy to bring the idea or creation to fruition. Finally nurturing is key in order to maintain the creation in a sustainable form.

Major birthing milestones are common in a three-year cycle to keep the relationship fresh and alive. The seasons of love and relationship cycles are explored further in chapter 6, yet for now a simple understanding on the importance of meeting each of the core needs is essential in moving your relationship forward. Whether it's choosing to have a child, moving in to a new home, or planning a holiday to a new location, the main point is that the two energies come together to invest in a common area of focus.

Identity (Uniqueness and Purpose)

The final element of the relationship plate of core needs is identity, defined by dictionary.com as "the condition of being oneself or itself and not another." This element is incredibly important as it ensures that your relationship is unique and serves each of you as individuals *and* as a whole. It provides freedom from any unresourceful efforts to tap into society's blueprint of what it means to be in a relationship and instead allows you to define your relationship as a couple based on your own unique needs and desires. People are drawn to those who are clear on what they are looking for in life, and successful role models can have a profound ripple effect. This core need is about living as a leader and change agent by getting clear on the identity of your relationship.

To create an identity for your relationship, you can begin by answering the following two questions:

1. What are the values and characteristics that support your relationship?
2. What is the overarching vision and purpose of your connection? What is it you want to achieve in your lifetime together?

Your responses to these questions are important for ensuring that your relationship is sustainable in a way that fulfills each individual and gives the relationship a purpose. Further questions on defining your relationship values were explored in chapter 2 and can support you in answering these questions on identity and purpose.

Lack of purpose is a common reason why many relationships fail. Often couples have not kept in touch with what it is they actually want out of life and what desired outcomes they want to achieve from their relationship. Too many people go about their everyday lives accepting whatever comes their way. If it's a good day, it's a good day. If bad things happen, it's a bad day. They take no responsibility for the results they are getting and let everything just kind of happen to them. "We fell out of love" is a common excuse for what really means "we weren't clear on where we were going and we are no longer on the same page."

Alternatively, if you have a relationship vision that outlines what it is you want to create in life, then you are more likely to move in that direction. You need to build your dreams first and then make sure those dreams become a reality by exploring the journey to achieve them. Of course, life is forever changing, and having a relationship vision or purpose is not about stamping out all levels of flexibility to create a checklist that must be strictly followed. Instead your purpose is likely to change and develop over the years as each of you grows on an individual and joint level. The important part is that you are continually checking in with each other and ensuring you have a relationship identity that remains true to who you are as individuals and as a couple. In a strong relationship you share a deep sense of meaning with your loved one. You don't just get along as part of daily interactions. You support each other's hopes, dreams, and aspirations and build a strong sense of purpose in your life together.

So in summary the four relationship needs are the following:

1. Friendship, where the connection of best friends keeps the relationship strong.
2. Love, where the role of lovers keeps the relationship alive with passion and fiery desire.

3. Creation, where the channeling of combined energy in the relationship is directed towards the growth of a fulfilling project external to the relationship.
4. Identity, where a unique relationship purpose is nurtured that serves both individuals and the relationship as a whole.

When one of the elements becomes neglected, frustration and unhappiness are inevitable, often sparking the breakdown of the relationship. For example, one of the key reasons relationships fail is that the creation element, the investment in the external, becomes the key focus of the relationship. In this situation the attention on the external and the archetype of the mother and father becomes so strong that the couple loses sight of the fact that they were once best friends who used to be lovers. Now all they focus on is the external creation, which often involves business or children. This is where you'll see relationships falling down very quickly. The important thing to remember is that none of these elements override the other. They are all required in order to create an ideal, balanced relationship.

**When a core need becomes neglected,
frustration and unhappiness are inevitable.**

Hayden and I travel a lot and have lived in several countries around the world. I can remember one specific time when we were packing up to leave Australia and move to Canada. We had our jobs and contracts to finish up, services and accounts to close, furniture and vehicles to sell, an apartment to clean, farewell coffee dates and dinners to attend, visa applications in process, study and assessments for an upcoming NLP training, tax returns to complete, a small business to run, trades to manage in a volatile market, a sick family member home in New Zealand, and a black-tie wedding to attend on our final weekend. One morning while we were packing up the apartment, I chose to indulge in some spectacular stress. It was impressive. There were its-all-too-much tears, slurred words from exhaustion, and a small amount of abuse towards the box I was packing at the time. Next came Hayden's profound solution to my stress. "I know what we need," he announced, and I waited eagerly for his words of wisdom to follow.

"We need to have more sex," he said.

While my old behaviour may have resembled complete shock and incredible frustration at his light-hearted, self-indulging approach to my stress, this time I realised he was right. So profound. The overinvestment in the external element—creation of a new life in Canada—was taking its toll on me and our relationship. We needed to bring the relationship plate of core needs back into balance. We had the creation element covered with moving to Canada, and the teamwork and best friend part was sorted as part of making things happen; however, the areas lacking were the passionate lover element and the connection with the bigger picture, the identity and purpose of the move. After we acknowledged our overcompensation in the external teamwork space, we quickly shifted our focus to a more balanced, light-hearted approach, including more sex and romance in between packing. The result was amazing. Suddenly we got more boxes packed and challenges sorted than we had previously been achieving. And it was so much more fun! We quickly become energised and reconnected with our bigger purpose and identity, reminding ourselves of our ultimate desire to explore the world and move to live in Canada.

By understanding the four core relationship needs, you can now begin to reflect on your own relationship. While you have been reading, you may have already begun to identify the areas in your own world where more focus is required. Take some time to discuss the different segments with your partner. Talk about the ways in which you meet the core needs of an ideal relationship within your own situation and perhaps brainstorm some ideas on how you might explore further ways to build upon the segments that may be lacking. The most common place to start is often a review and rebuild of the best friend segment of the relationship. Best friends will do whatever their best friend needs to be happy, providing a strong foundation for a relationship rebuild. Best friends are founded on trust, which can then begin the rebuild of the love/passion, creation, and identity elements. Approach the conversation with your partner with trust and understanding always.

Chapter Summary

At their core many conflicts within a relationship are really a conflict between different core needs. When you zoom out and reflect on each of the needs and the way in which they are being met in your own life and within your relationship, then you can begin to identify specific areas of satisfaction, challenge, and desired improvement. When you create an extensive list of resourceful vehicles that meet each of your core needs, then you have a recipe for fulfillment. The more resourceful strategies you have for meeting each of these core needs, the better.

When it comes to setting the table in preparation for a meal, there are key tools required. Knives and forks are the dominant table tools embraced in the Western world, while chopsticks are the defining tools of the Asian population. In India it is tradition to eat with your fingers, where food is often scooped onto flatbread, such as naan and roti, to be transported to the mouth. Tools vary across the world yet serve the same purpose. In the same way the tools reflected in this chapter vary yet combine to serve the purpose of increasing the success in your relationship. The "Exercises for Reflection" section will give you the full benefit of this model in terms of its ability to identify specific areas of focus and improvement in your own life right now.

Exercises for Reflection

Exploring Your Relationship Plate of Core Needs

How would you rate your satisfaction surrounding each of the core needs discussed in this chapter on a scale of one to ten, where ten is the highest level? Complete the following exercise on your own and then come together with your partner to discuss your thoughts and share each of your answers. Remember to approach your reflection conversation with trust and understanding always.

Individual Core Needs

Needs of the Personality

Certainty (Security and Comfort)

- How would you rate your satisfaction surrounding your need for certainty based on your access to resourceful, high-quality vehicles?

  1   2   3   4   5   6   7   8   9   10

- What key things in your life right now currently meet your need for certainty in a resourceful way?

- How does your relationship meet your need for certainty?

- Do you have any unresourceful vehicles you have identified for meeting your need for certainty?

- What learning points or areas of improvement would you like to see in this category?

- What new actions are you now committed to taking?

Variety (Challenges and Adventure)

- How would you rate your satisfaction surrounding your need for variety based on your access to resourceful, high-quality vehicles?

  1   2   3   4   5   6   7   8   9   10

- What key things in your life right now currently meet your need for variety in a resourceful way?

- How does your relationship meet your need for variety?

- Do you have any unresourceful vehicles you have identified for meeting your need for variety?

- What learning points or areas of improvement would you like to see in this category?

- What new actions are you now committed to taking?

Significance (Important, Special and Unique)

- How would you rate your satisfaction surrounding your need for significance based on your access to resourceful, high-quality vehicles?

  1   2   3   4   5   6   7   8   9   10

- What key things in your life right now currently meet your need for significance in a resourceful way?

- How does your relationship meet your need for significance?

- Do you have any unresourceful vehicles you have identified for meeting your need for significance?

- What learning points or areas of improvement would you like to see in this category?

- What new actions are you now committed to taking?

Love and Connection (Approval and Attachment)

- How would you rate your satisfaction surrounding your need for love and connection based on your access to resourceful, high-quality vehicles?

  1   2   3   4   5   6   7   8   9   10

- What key things in your life right now currently meet your need for love and connection in a resourceful way?

- How does your relationship meet your need for love and connection?

- Do you have any unresourceful vehicles you have identified for meeting your need for love and connection?

- What learning points or areas of improvement would you like to see in this category?

- What new actions are you now committed to taking?

Needs of the Spirit

Growth (Progress and Development)

- How would you rate your satisfaction surrounding your need for growth based on your access to resourceful, high-quality vehicles?

    1   2   3   4   5   6   7   8   9   10

- What key things in your life right now currently meet your need for growth in a resourceful way?

- How does your relationship meet your need for growth?

- Do you have any unresourceful vehicles you have identified for meeting your need for growth?

- What learning points or areas of improvement would you like to see in this category?

- What new actions are you now committed to taking?

Contribution (Service to Others)

- How would you rate your satisfaction surrounding your need for contribution based on your access to resourceful, high-quality vehicles?

  1   2   3   4   5   6   7   8   9   10

- What key things in your life right now currently meet your need for contribution in a resourceful way?

- How does your relationship meet your need for contribution?

- Do you have any unresourceful vehicles you have identified for meeting your need for contribution?

- What learning points or areas of improvement would you like to see in this category?

- What new actions are you now committed to taking?

Relationship Core Needs

Friendship (Best Friends and Strength)

- How would you rate your satisfaction surrounding the friendship element of your relationship?

  1   2   3   4   5   6   7   8   9   10

- What key things in your relationship right now currently meet the core need for friendship (best friends and strength)?

- How could you work with your partner to make the levels of satisfaction in this category even higher right now? What specific things might you introduce to your relationship?

Love (Lovers and Passion)

- How would you rate your satisfaction surrounding the love and passion element of your relationship?

  1   2   3   4   5   6   7   8   9   10

- What key things in your relationship right now currently meet the core need for love (lovers and passion)?

- How could you work with your partner to make the levels of satisfaction in this category even higher right now? What specific things might you introduce to your relationship?

Creation (Parents and Fulfillment)

- How would you rate your satisfaction surrounding the creation element of your relationship?

  1   2   3   4   5   6   7   8   9   10

- What key things in your relationship right now currently meet the core need for creation (parents and fulfillment)?

- How could you work with your partner to make the levels of satisfaction in this category even higher right now? What specific things might you introduce to your relationship?

Identity (Uniqueness and Purpose)

- How would you rate your satisfaction surrounding the identity element of your relationship?

  1   2   3   4   5   6   7   8   9   10

- What key things in your relationship right now currently meet the core need for identity (uniqueness and purpose)?

- How could you work with your partner to make the levels of satisfaction in this category even higher right now? What specific things might you introduce to your relationship?

Chapter 4

The Special Touch on Setting the Table: Exploring Feminine Energy

Feminine essence in men and women
is expressed through the power of unity,
connection, and relationship.

My friend calls me from her super-yacht job in the Caribbean. She and her man are employed to serve the richer members of society on flashy yachts in some of the most stunning locations throughout the world. Having left the corporate scene to pursue an adventure at sea, she calls to tell me she is worried.

"I spend my days cleaning and ironing. And I love it," she tells me. "Yet how can ironing and caring for others be so satisfying? I just don't get it. I feel so at home as I work my way around the boat, cleaning and caring for every little speck and spot. I can get a stain out of anything," she tells me proudly and laughs.

I smile as I acknowledge the shift I hear in her voice. She really does sound a lot more relaxed and at peace.

"Yet I cry a lot," she shares. "While a part of me loves the simplicity and deep sense of connection I get from caring for the team, another part of me feels like I should be doing more and striving for a bigger purpose like the professional status I left behind in the corporate world. Who am I now? A professional cleaner for the rich and famous?"

It suddenly dawns on me that what my friend is sharing has a major theme that rests between the tension of masculine and feminine energy. While her love, energy, and flow—feminine side—feels safe and satisfied with the role she is playing at sea, her masculine side is demanding purpose, direction, competition, and drive.

This balance between *being* (as feminine) and *doing* (as masculine) can often create a conflict in our everyday lives in a form that many of us fail to recognise. As a result, the conflict and disharmony that is created when either the masculine or feminine energy is out of balance results in internal struggles. Naturally these internal struggles continue to transpire through difficulties in a relationship context, given our relationships are also a complementary balance of the two opposing energies. A lot of what my friend continued to share that day as we talked through her challenges reflected a shift towards the feminine energy. The focus of her attention had moved away from her endless to-do lists in the corporate world to a focus that was more internal, looking inside the body to become present with the moment. My friend's removal from everyday life to an in-the-moment experience out at sea allowed her to reconnect with her feminine sense of being. Yet after some time this reconnection came with a side impact of guilt and a sense of loss connected with her previously very strong masculine presence. This is a common by-product during the process of reconnecting with self, where the perceived sense of guilt arises because many of us are not familiar with what it means to exist in the moment. In fact, we live in a society so attuned to the masculine form of production that we very rarely stop to reflect on the level of thinking you are about to explore throughout the next two chapters.

One of the most important things you can do to improve your chances of success in your relationship is to become educated about the differences between men and woman. As part of that education the concepts of masculine and feminine energy must be explored because if you can grasp these concepts and understand the characteristics of these two energies, then you can apply this level of thinking to your own life and relationship with your loved one to reveal profound insights.

To improve your chances of success in your relationship, it's essential to become educated about the differences between men and woman.

Masculine and feminine energy does not refer to the specific sex of females and males but rather the energetic states or forces of creation. Both masculine and feminine energy exists within all of us, and the goal is to balance these energies to create oneness. Naturally a man will have more masculine energy and vice versa for a female, yet it is important to note that the energies do not determine gender and instead simply influence behaviour. There are also exceptions to these natural states, and nothing is set in concrete. To explain this concept further, this chapter introduces masculine and feminine energy through an understanding of the yin and yang model, an energy theory central to Taoism. It then goes on to apply this learning to a relationship context, exploring why strong women often attract weak men, how to connect with your feminine essence, and the impacts of living in a predominantly masculine world. While some parts of this chapter are written in a context specifically for females, I would encourage men to take note as well, approaching the topic with an open mind and understanding that feminine energy exists within all of us and that all insights serve both sexes.

The metaphor of "special touch on setting the table" can most certainly be portrayed in physical artifacts—where the flowers are strategically arranged, the cutlery is matching, and the ambience is set with candles, mood lighting, and appropriate background music—yet this chapter and element of the kitchen table model is more importantly about the bigger picture and connection with the feminine essence. It is this connection with the feminine essence that drives the ambience and energy of love and flow within the environment—the surroundings that makes the table setting unique and special. The feminine energy sets the atmosphere for dining and is the secret touch that makes a house a home.

Yin and Yang: Introducing Masculine and Feminine Energy

It is helpful to think of masculine and feminine energy in terms of yin and yang, a theory central to Taoism and traditional Chinese medicine that states the world is made up of two opposing yet complementary forces. In this philosophy the two forces work together to create harmony and order in our natural world. When these two qualities are out of balance, resistance and disorder occurs. The two pieces are vital components working in equal nature to create balance and sustainability, and many natural dualities are thought of as yin and yang respectively—dark and light, low and high, cold and hot, and female and male.

When masculine and feminine energy are out of balance, resistance and disorder occurs.

To further understand these dualities, a review of the yin and yang symbol is an ideal place to start, as it provides a beautiful platform for learning about the intimate connection between the two energies. To begin, let's take a closer look at the formation of the yin-yang symbol.

Firstly the outer circle of the image represents the Tao or the single principle from which everything else is derived. This circle is then divided into two opposite components that interact with each other—yin, the black half, and yang, the white half. These two components ignite everything and encompass the changes in the universe through the five elements of wood, earth, fire, water, and metal. Taoism explains the workings of the universe through the yin-and-yang interactions of the five agents as they interchange, oppose, merge, yield to, overcome, birth, and feed off one another. The interaction of the two opposing components is illustrated through a flowing dissection where each half appears to be in constant movement, cycling into the next through the illustration of the flowing curve. The Taoist principles detail that each of the components nourishes, sustains, and controls the other, and each depends upon the other to exist. The sides are therefore described as complementary rather than absolutes.

The next key element to note as part of the constantly moving opposites is the inclusion of balance and equilibrium. In each of the coloured halves we see a small circle of the opposite colour. Again this element reinforces that there are no absolutes in the yin-and-yang theory. Instead this illustration emphasises that in every yang there is a little yin and that in every yin there is a little yang. They are not only reflections of each other but are reflected *in* each other. In the same way, in every light there is a little dark. In every high there is a little low, and in every evil there is a little good. It's as if each half sees the other through the eye of its complementary opposite. One energy is not better or supposed to dominate the other. Rather, they work in flow, where the raw energy or pressure (masculine) meets the passive and receptive force (feminine) that brings about creation. They know each other well.

At a closer look, yin energy refers to the feminine, encompassing traditional characteristics including:

- winter
- dark
- passive
- receptive
- soft
- downward
- cold
- water
- earth
- moon

Yang energy refers to the masculine, including traditional interpretations:

- summer
- light
- active
- directive
- hard
- upward
- hot
- fire
- sky
- sun

To add to these insights, more contemporary interpretations of the yin-and-yang theory define feminine as the following:

- internal
- shadow
- Mother Earth
- nature
- feeling
- intuition
- attraction
- collective
- flexible
- flow
- process
- sustainability

Masculine traits include the following:

- external
- transcendence
- Father Spirit
- culture
- thinking
- logic
- assertion
- individual
- rigid

- go
- outcome
- peak experience

To add to these characteristics, yin refers to the feminine energy as the negative magnetic pole that works with attraction as opposed to assertion with the yang pole. If you think of the act of sex, the female is open and receptive to penetration, attracting the physical act towards her and inwards of her body. Alternatively the male embraces assertion and direction towards the feminine. Of course, all these generalisations are open to further interpretation and are simply what I have found to be the best descriptions to begin to explore the two components of masculine and feminine.

The characteristics of these energies can be used to describe individuals, environments, countries, and working cultures. For example, a workplace environment can be described as having either a dominant masculine or feminine feel. Countries can also be described in this same way. People tend to move slower in Hawaii, where the feminine energy is very alive and the focus is on island time, embracing the emotional flow of daily events. In a predominantly feminine culture the emphasis is on the quality of life in respect to the environment. As a comparison, downtown Chicago moves at a much faster pace with a very masculine environment where productivity and ambition are highly valued.

The exploration of masculine and feminine energy as part of the *Love on the Kitchen Table* model will be gender-specific in line with the natural state of males drawing on more of their masculine energy and females drawing on more of their femininity. I trust you will then translate your learning into the context of your own energy balance, knowing that both energies exist within you always. My intention is to introduce you to masculine and feminine energy in a summarised context that will have the biggest possible impact in your life right now. Should you become hooked—and I trust you will—then further exploration and study on masculine and feminine energy is well worth your time.

The Impact of Energy Balance on Relationships

The beauty of balance becomes evident when you reflect on the impact of masculine and feminine energy in a relationship context where the two complementary components work together to create harmony. Each side nourishes, sustains, and controls the other, and each depends upon the other to exist. What this means in the context of a relationship is that the two pieces are vital and must exist in a harmonious balance in order to embrace functional flow. The control element highlights the complementary nature of the two energies. A high masculine force will attract a high feminine force to achieve equilibrium and vice versa. For example, men with high masculine traits will attract females with the complementary balance—lower masculine and higher feminine traits. Author David Deida explains how you always attract your reciprocal energy. "A woman who worships a man's depth of masculine consciousness attracts and inspires a man who worships her heart of devotional feminine radiance."

Yet challenges arise when this dynamic shifts away from the natural state. For example, females with strong masculine characteristics will naturally attract men with lower masculinity and stronger feminine traits. While on rare occasions this flow may be functional for a period of time, the dynamics go against the natural state of males and females, and therefore, you will likely see an increase in dissonance and conflict within the relationship. She will often expect her man to step up or man up in his role as the male because at her core this is what she's looking for—a strong man. Yet what she doesn't realise is that she is dominating this masculine space, where the complementary nature of the yin-and-yang model keeps him held in the feminine space if the balance is to work.

A high masculine force will attract a high feminine force to achieve equilibrium.

Think about the masculine and feminine energy balance as a pie graph. If she has 70 per cent feminine energy with 30 per cent masculine, then this leaves a complementary space for a male with the opposite flow of 70 per cent masculine energy and 30 per cent feminine. Both parties are dominantly in their natural states, and the balance can be described as a harmonious flow. When the balance moves away from the natural state, this is where we begin to experience relationship conflict. There are different scenarios that commonly play out as a result of this imbalance. Firstly if both partners have high masculine tendencies, they will compete for space like bulls in a fight arena. You may recognise this behaviour in parts of your own relationship history, or you may have witnessed it within the relationships of people you know, where both dominant personalities are constantly fighting for space. In this instance, it is likely the arguments and conflict will eventually cause the breakdown of the relationship unless one of the partners actively chooses to embrace more of the feminine to allow the connection to exist in harmony. If she chooses to embrace the feminine, then the natural state is restored. Alternatively if he really wants the relationship to work, he may take on the more feminine traits to allow her to exist in her masculine. Because this scenario goes against the grain of the natural states, over time she will likely experience immense stress and a feeling of disconnect with self as a result of living with consistently high masculine characteristics. On an unconscious level she will be yearning for her need to connect with her feminine emotional flow and her sense of being. Females define their sense of self by the quality of their relationships, and therefore, a task-focused, logical, masculine approach to life can become very exhausting and unsatisfying. You can't describe love in a strategic plan. Yet the majority of the time she won't realise that it's this prolonged focus on masculine traits that are causing her to feel stressed. On an unconscious level she will find ways to test her man and demand that he steps up to fulfill the masculine role. You'll see arguments that begin with "why didn't you take out the trash?" and end with her saying, "That's it. We're over." Yet the real issue is that there is no space for him to step up, as she is dominating the masculine energy in the household, and therefore, she will only ever be able to attract a boy-man who fits with her flow of strong masculine energy.

"The hard driving woman has to switch persona when she gets home. She's got to throttle back, or she'll castrate everything in the domestic niche. Many white, middle-class women have dodged this dilemma by finding themselves a nice, malleable boy-man who becomes another son in the subliminally matriarchal household," writes Robert Glover in his work *No More Mr. Nice Guy*. What she craves is a strong, masculine man. This topic of "why females test their men" is covered further in chapter 5, yet for now it's essential to understand the profound impact the energy balance has on our relationships when the balance is moved away from the natural state.

In comparison to the feminine link to love and relationships, males define their sense of self by the accomplishment and connection with their vision and purpose, which is unique for each individual. If they are not connected with this sense of purpose, they can become incredibly demotivated and unsatisfied. Again this purpose is supported by the natural masculine traits of direction, focus, and decision-making. Masculine energy is explored more in chapter 5.

Given the insights you are now gaining, you can begin to reflect on the current balance in your own world and the impact within your own relationship. If you are to think of your energy like a pie graph, what percentage of feminine versus masculine traits do you feel you portray in your life right now? Given your relationship creates a complementary opposite, what does this presuppose about your partner? Is this balance in your relationship currently functional, or are there areas you can work on to create a more harmonious balance that best serves you both?

Your reflection on your own connection with each of the energies should include your childhood imprinting phase. As an overview, you learned the flow of love in relationships from your mother, your primary role model in the space of feminine energy. You then learned the value of decisions, direction, and action from your father, your primary role model in the space of masculine energy. With this in mind, when I have clients who talk about starting their own businesses (ideas and creations of the feminine) yet face challenges with achieving financial results (actions, directions, and achievements of the masculine), then I begin our discussion with a focus on their relationships with their fathers. Alternatively when I have clients who are struggling with their relationships and ability to show affection, then we explore their relationships with their mothers. The insights provided within these characteristic sets are incredibly powerful in terms of understanding human behaviour, and when actively applied to your own world, they can help you move and shape your life to your desired form.

While the masculine and feminine energies within us are very different, it is important to understand they are supposed to work in harmony. One energy is not better or supposed to dominate the other. You cannot have just feminine energy or just masculine energy, but the ideal is to combine the gifts of both in order to be whole. This is because polarities, without losing their meaning and integrity, find fulfillment and realisation in integration. In her work *Liberating Masculine and Feminine*, author Rosemarie Carnarius talks of the beauty that is created as part of this integration of both the masculine and feminine, where "in their union a third element, a new creation, emerges, inclusive of both, yet favoring neither."

Females and Feminine Energy

At her core nature a woman feels much more pleasure when her feminine essence is primary. Her personal power and magnetism grows when she chooses to connect with her feminine core and when she looks inward to her physical, emotional, and energetic body to guide her. Operating with a feminine essence can also be described as waiting for the right time to make a decision without the need to rush ahead. If it were swimming, it would be breaststroke. If it were a dance, it would be interpretive. And if it were a drink, I'd say it's a warm herbal tea. The rhythm of the feminine is slower than the usual pace people move at, guided more by the sensual beat of life as opposed to the need to forge ahead. Characterised by feelings, this energy is the creative and receptive power of unity, connection, and relationship, which weaves all of creation together.

At her core nature a woman feels much more pleasure when her feminine essence is primary.

As we delve deeper into what it means to be feminine, it is essential we address the limiting belief within society that the feminine power is the weaker of the two energies. This is far from the truth. I believe the issue here arises from a global perception that strength is outside of us. As an example, the *World English Dictionary* defines strength as "the state or quality of being physically or mentally strong; the ability to withstand or exert great force, stress or pressure." Our perception of strength positions it outside of us with descriptions of physical pressure and the ability to withstand great force. The reference to mental strength refers to logic and remaining mentally strong, once again a masculine trait of left-brain thinking. This state of strength is glorified as a preferred characteristic, and upon review of this definition of strength it becomes obvious how over time the feminine energy has come to be viewed as the weaker of the two energies. Yet in order to reconnect with the feminine, we must shift our thinking to acknowledge the innate strength that exists within the feminine realm. While external strength is associated with the masculine energy, the strength associated with the feminine can be describe as more of an internal strength powered by emotional intelligence from the heart space. As opposed to assertion and direction, this strength is characterised by vulnerability and openness. A woman in her feminine essence knows the power of vulnerability, and she is open to receive in the most pure, loving sense. She is connected physically, emotionally, and spiritually with the power of her womb, and she celebrates what it means to be a woman. Before she walks into any room, all she has to do is choose to feel her compassionate nature, harnessing the certainty within her that whatever the moment calls for, she has it within her right now. Her state of being allows her to draw on the true essence of the moment, to create a beauty of unity and connection. This internal feminine power of vulnerability and openness is incredibly strong, and in order to move forward and become connected with

,

celebrating the feminine, we must choose to celebrate both the external and internal characteristics of strength.

Living in the space of emotion and love allows you to operate with an inner sense of peace, knowing that when you show up, you have all the resources you need within you always. The feminine flow also allows a deeper connection through the relationships in your world, enhancing the quality of your day-to-day interactions with those around you and ultimately contributing to your own sense of self-worth. Author Marianne Williamson says, "Feminine power isn't something we go out and acquire; it's already within us. It's something we become willing to experience. Something to admit we have."

In connecting with your own feminine essence, have a think about the relationship you currently have with your body. How much time do you spend celebrating what it means to be female? For example, how would you describe your relationship with your womb? This may sound odd, but this incredibly spiritual and sacred space must command respect when it comes to embracing your feminine essence. Too often we are bombarded with messages from the media that tell us to plug up and carry on during the period of menstruating. We are told a tampon can fix anything, allowing you to immediately get back to work. As a result of this very masculine, task-focused approach to the reproductive system, many women today have become completely disconnected with their bodies and monthly cycles. The menstrual cycle is often viewed as an inconvenience, which many seek to regulate through contraceptive means, once again embracing the masculine need to control. My intent in referring to these topics is not to put a right or wrong label on items like tampons or the contraceptive pill but instead to raise your awareness surrounding the underlying messages driving the advertising and acceptance of these items. It's messages like these that impact your relationship with the feminine.

I once heard a speaker in this area describe the menstrual cycle as a "monthly release of lost potential." She referred to the process as a spiritual and truly magical example of the body's ability to create life and self-regulate. As I look back, my initial reaction to her words were fascinating. I was so shocked at her description of the feminine cycle, which so blatantly drew attention to the body's amazing ability to create life. Why the shock? Well, as I reflect back, I guess it was not often that I had heard people speak of the menstrual cycle in such a natural, pure, and loving way, appreciating it for the great ability to create new life. As women, whether we choose to have children or not is beside the point. Regardless, the menstrual cycle itself and the ability of the body to procreate is a symbol of something magical and incredibly powerful—one that should not be swept under the rug.

During my period of menstruation Hayden would often say, "Oh, it's *that* time of the month. You're no good to me this week," complete with a wicked and cheeky smile.

While his words were meant as a light-hearted joke, what they fundamentally represent is a sense of *brokenness* or *not working* or *hindrance* that creates inferiority. His words also mirrored my own frustration at the time when I viewed my cycle as an inconvenience on everyday life. Quite the paradox really. Following my own work I've now done on connecting with my feminine power, I no longer buy into these limiting beliefs that are so often sold to us in mainstream media and filtered through the beliefs of common thinking. Instead I now actively choose to celebrate what it means to be feminine—and it makes the world of difference—rather than attempt to control my cycle or complain at its arrival. I also take careful notice of the signs my body shares during each stage of my own personal, rhythmic flow, and I embrace the feelings of my womb and ovaries in action. I choose to actively acknowledge the "monthly release of lost potential" in a special, loving way, and if I feel low on energy, then I allow myself to rest in that space as opposed to plugging up and continuing with my to-do list. For me, it has become all about choosing to embrace what my body needs in the moment, whether it's a hot bath, yoga, some quiet time, a walk through nature, or some extra rest. There is no right or wrong, no good or bad, simply what is true for me at the time. I've learnt that this is ultimately what feminine flow refers to, which allows love to guide your daily sense of being. This feminine flow must not trigger emotions of guilt. You need no rhyme or reason to just be and exist in the moment based on what you feel.

꙰

Feminine flow allows love to guide
your daily sense of being.

꙰

While I was writing this chapter, I witnessed an ad on TV that further emphasised this point. A promotion for an indigestion drug delivered a sing-song message that stated, "Now you can eat whatever you want," alongside a series of images, including cheesy nachos, a greasy burger, and chicken wings, completed by an audio track of satisfied burps. The message presupposed that despite the body's reaction to these foods, through the assistance of the recommended drug you could simply block the symptoms of indigestion and carry on eating whatever your heart desired. What the ad failed to explore is the reason *why* your body may be reacting in this way to these particular foods. Perhaps the body is not supposed to be able to easily absorb an excessive amount of these types of food, yet the ad leads you to embrace a "block it up and carry on" approach that's very much focused on action, results, and moving forward. Alternatively a more feminine approach would be to stop, reflect, and look inwards to the body to guide your emotion towards what's going on and to then act based on the messages from the body.

In addition to exploring the emotional characteristics of femininity and the connection with the body, a reflection on the look of feminine energy in today's society is equally fascinating.

This reflection can only really be based on the perceived appearance of femininity, as perceptions differ among different individuals and take on new characteristics across cultural borders. With this in mind and with the intention to trigger more of your own personal thinking in this space, I will focus on the feminine look in the Western world. Beginning with the top of the body, the perception of femininity includes long or soft hairstyles, usually with hair out and softening the shape of the face. To complement the softness of the hair, long eyelashes are also regarded as highly feminine. Next the application of make-up works to add colour, and the flushing of the cheeks creates a warm sense of rapport. Working down the body, the typical feminine outfit will accentuate the shape of the body, specifically focusing on breasts, the buttocks, and legs. These body parts and their link to femininity and attraction are explored further in chapter 9, yet for now it is important to note the way in which they are accentuated in the Western world as part of a feminine look. Soft and flowing materials are also often connected with femininity and can include patterns or details of creativity. Accessories, specifically jewellery, are worn as symbols and gifts of love, unity, and connection, all very feminine characteristics.

It is also interesting to look at the contrast of masculine dress when females choose to take on a more masculine look. In this instance, accessories take on the symbol of external power, and the dress characteristics resemble direction, action, and purpose.

Take the female corporate suit for example. Usually dark in colour, with sharp lines and a strict collar that outlines the neck, the corporate suit is incredibly masculine in its form. The sharp lines create a look of decisiveness and the unspoken message is this: "I mean business." Hair pulled back in to a tight ponytail can often complement the suit look, adding to the masculinity of the outfit. Outside of the office space and as part of daily living, bulky boots and hardy clothing that resemble trade or labour can also be termed masculine in the Western world. These thicker items suggest protection from a physical task requiring external strength, again typically in the masculine space.

While these generalisations are intended to get you thinking about the look of femininity, they also provide a starting point to explore this concept further and to discuss it with your loved one. Does he prefer hair up or hair down? Does he prefer soft hair that shapes the face or hair that is tightly pulled back in a ponytail? What specific items of clothing does he find attractive? These types of questions can ignite a conversation that will further work to define what it means to look feminine.

A long-time-single mother came to me with a range of life challenges, including her desire to attract a strong, masculine man into her life. While we explored a range of topics to move her towards this goal, of particular note was the work we did around masculine and feminine energy. The pattern we identified in her world was the continued attraction of weak men into her life. She felt that the men she dated constantly failed her and were unable to make decisions, provide direction, or take action to move the relationship forward. Basically they lacked the strong, masculine traits she was looking for. In our coaching sessions we explored the dynamics of a complementary masculine and feminine energy balance, and we talked about her role as a single mother. She felt her daily tasks required her to adopt a strong masculine façade in order to protect both her and her son. As part of this insight she realised that by adopting a masculine façade she was blocking the space in her life for a strong, masculine energy to enter, as she already had this area covered. We explored this impact of her high masculine energy as part of her attraction strategy, and she expressed the desire to get back in touch with her feminine side in order to then attract a strong man. We began by actively seeking ways to get in touch with what it meant to be feminine, and we started with the physical artifacts of her wardrobe. When I asked her to describe the contents of her wardrobe, she had two items for me—polo shirts and jeans with the addition of a denim skirt that she rotated in the summer with the polo shirt to match. Following this discussion our next coaching session took place in her bedroom with the wardrobe doors fully open. We talked about the emotions that were attached to the articles of clothing and the feelings that came up when she wore each piece. Surprisingly at the back of the wardrobe and behind all the jeans and polo shirts, there were some incredibly feminine items, many with the price tag still in place. We pulled all items out and put them on the bed to reflect on each outfit choice and explore the attached emotions and intention behind the look of each piece. As part of the exploration, she acknowledged that the jeans and polo shirt combination provided a feeling of safety, comfort, and an under-the-radar approach to not being noticed. The clothing also reinforced some underlying beliefs around not being good enough for positive attention from the opposite sex. When she dressed in a way that kept her safe, she reinforced to her unconscious mind that she was unworthy of attention and love. We continued to explore the emotions attached to the more feminine items of clothing—the ones with the price tags still in place. There were some limiting beliefs related to attracting unwanted attention and always putting herself second. Once again we worked through these limitations to move in the direction of her desired goal to reconnect with her feminine side. The process was incredible. After hours of exploration we'd worked through the symbols and emotions attached with each item in her wardrobe, and she chose to only return items to the wardrobe that she felt would manifest the results she desired. Changes to the physical items in your wardrobe are one of the quickest ways to reconnect with your feminine side, and the effect can be very powerful. Two weeks later I got a gorgeous email from her talking about the impact she'd noticed in her world as a ripple effect of introducing more feminine items to her everyday attire. "It's incredible. I've noticed an improvement in my relationship with my three-year-old son and noticed changes in his behaviour too. Friends have commented that I have a calm aura and that I am the happiest they have ever seen me. They are right, and I feel great!"

It's not really about the clothing. Instead it's the beliefs and emotions that exist in the space of connection with the feminine. It's this connection that must also be understood through its innate relationship to the masculine. There is no purely feminine woman or no wholly masculine man; both energies must be valued and respected. As author Rosemarie Carnarius writes in her work *Liberating Masculine and Feminine*,

> Because yin and yang, feminine and masculine, are essential components of existence, which participate each moment in the shaping of our individual and collective lives, it is incumbent upon us to gain a true understanding of their nature and dynamics in order to be liberated from the prison of our ignorance. This requires recognizing polarities as co-creative partners, instead of perceiving them as opposites and antagonists.

Living in a Masculine World

In chapter 1 we looked briefly at a changing environment in terms of beliefs and explored the reality of living in a world that often glorifies divorce with a lack of backing towards marriage. A continued reflection on the world in which we live is equally important when we choose to explore the depths of masculine and feminine energy. Again the 1960s marks a prominent milestone in society with the awakening of woman towards an impulse and desire to level the playing field between man and woman. In this quest to embrace a more equal lifestyle, a lot of positive things came about. We experienced enormous advances where woman became autonomous, gained increased education, and embraced a standard of living and freedom beyond the wildest dreams of our great-grandmothers. At the same time the joint masculine push in society saw the marvels of industry reach a whole new level, and the miracles of science took humanity to a new and unrecognised place. Yet with all of this in mind, what must be acknowledged are the characteristics that have moved us through this phase. Direction, production, and action have characterised our world over the last few decades, where achievement has been viewed as outside of our bodies in a tangible, structural form. The fast-paced advances in society have also introduced specific challenges. In her book *Powerful and Feminine*, Rachael Jayne Groover talks about the pattern over recent centuries, where we have distanced ourselves away from the feminine energy to create a heavily masculine society focused on competition, development, and results. She writes, "We have come to a point in history where the consequences of disowning the feminine are becoming apparent in painful, frightening ways: climate change, war, a global economic crises, as well as an overall lack of passion and purpose are just a few of the major costs."

I must emphasise here that this focus on destruction is *not* attributed to males but instead to the masculine traits that exist within both males and females. These are the traits that have been celebrated and glorified as the more powerful and preferred qualities for some time. It's fascinating to witness the impact on our relationships. When we have a world full of bulls in a ring, each fighting to achieve an external sense of power and achievement, it begins to make sense that in conjunction with the physical impact on the world, divorce numbers are at an all-time high.

Yet in the process what specifically have we sacrificed? According to a 2007 report from the National Bureau of Economic Research, "as women have gained more freedom, more education, and more power, they have become *less* happy." In the pursuit of equality and power, many women have chosen to take on a more masculine role in their desire to be strong and independent. Yet as a by-product of this shift, they have also begun to shut themselves off from their softness, sensuality, and feminine energy, all of the characteristics that bring pleasure to the feminine core and that increase inner radiance. While we have experienced many advances as part of a global masculine movement, we are now also experiencing the complementary impacts. The overcompensation in the masculine space has left us now asking more about what it is we *actually* want to achieve in life. I believe we are now experiencing a renaissance and yearning questions are awakening. When we reflect on the yin-yang theory, what we are seeing is a global shift from what has been a very masculine world towards a desire to connect with the feminine. And in fact, it is this yearning of the feminine that I would argue solves the mystery as to why many women are experiencing a sense of something missing in their lives right now—a common message I hear in my coaching work. As a result, what we are witnessing is more women than ever before starting up their own businesses and choosing lives directed more towards love, intimacy, meaning, and contribution, lives where we as women are asking ourselves a fundamental question about how we can contribute to the world in a more meaningful way.

To begin to create the things we yearn for as women, we need to cultivate a new power system from that which we have pushed towards as part of the three waves of feminism. Instead, we are now looking inside of ourselves to connect with the co-creative feminine power, focusing on those things that can't necessarily be controlled by external power. We are realising that our relationships match and mirror the truth of who we are, and we are no longer prepared to settle for mediocrity. Instead we are looking for ways to contribute to a bigger picture, and we are seeing the pendulum swing to a focus on mankind's impact on our environment, including a deeper appreciation of our planet, our communities, our relationships, the way we live, and the quality of the food we choose to put in our bodies.

**Our relationships match and mirror
the truth of who we are.**

I share these thoughts with you to fuel your own sense of thinking and reflection on your world around you right now. I know when I was first exposed to this level of thinking, I noticed the deeper sense of connection that existed within me—my feminine side—and actively chose to connect with it. It's like the knowledge gave me permission to embrace some of the key emotions and associated activities I had been previously sweeping under the rug. Firstly I began working on getting clear about my own beliefs, values, and the way in which I choose to live my life. I sought a way that I could harness my creative energy and serve the world around me in a form of contribution—communications, coaching, and writing. I also began to take an increased interest in my daily activities, ensuring they were in alignment with my goals. I began to exercise in a way that aligned with my body's rhythm and become more conscious about the foods I was putting in my body. As part of this transition, I also became more aware of where my food came from and the specific array of ingredients, distance from source, and impact on the environment. This thinking comes from a place of consideration for both myself and the world around me.

The pendulum is swaying back to an increased respect for the feminine. We are evolving beyond patterns external to us to realise our true potential. We are harnessing the ability to co-create, and in doing so, we are attracting the power of the collective field of support. It is this collective field of support that creates the uniqueness of "the special touch on setting the table" metaphor. It is the ambience, support, and internal power that exists in the space of nurturance.

Chapter Summary

Without having a solid understanding of the biological, emotional, and spiritual make-up of men and women, including a strong understanding of masculine and feminine energy, it is often very difficult to sustain relationships. It's the environment that is created, where in an effortless flow the transitions between masculine and feminine energy are seamless; however, when the energies are out of balance, pain arises, and the disconnect quickly becomes visible to the naked eye.

Exercises for Reflection

Following your reflection on feminine energy throughout this chapter, explore the following questions to further embed your learning and relevance to your own world right now.

1. If you think of your energy like a pie graph, what percentage of feminine versus masculine traits do you feel you portray in your life right now?

2. What specific evidence tells you this balance is true?

3. How does this balance play out in your relationship right now?

4. While you were exploring this chapter, what specific things have you identified that you would like to change to assist you in reaching your relationship goals?

5. What has been the biggest gift in reading this chapter for you personally?

Take the Quiz: How Feminine Are You?

The following questions are designed to get you thinking about the nature of femininity and to gauge your own current connection with your feminine essence. Respond to each of the questions based on the level at which you feel you relate to the statement, where one equals "I don't relate at all" and ten equals "I completely relate to this statement."

1. I often take a moment to purposefully reflect on how I am feeling about a certain topic or situation.

   1   2   3   4   5   6   7   8   9   10

2. I express my emotions outwardly, including when I am experiencing sadness or pain.

   1   2   3   4   5   6   7   8   9   10

3. I often receive intuitive signs or messages that I actively follow through on, trusting the flow of my environment.

   1   2   3   4   5   6   7   8   9   10

4. I prefer to work in teams and to have access to other creative minds in order to fuel my own development and growth.

   1   2   3   4   5   6   7   8   9   10

5. I believe we cannot become ourselves by ourselves.

   1   2   3   4   5   6   7   8   9   10

6. Intimate relationships are incredibly important to me.

   1   2   3   4   5   6   7   8   9   10

7. Having an aesthetically beautiful home and garden is important to me.

   1   2   3   4   5   6   7   8   9   10

8. I am actively involved in my local community and place strong importance on networking with others.

   1   2   3   4   5   6   7   8   9   10

9. I prefer it when my partner makes the decisions about where to go on a date night and am always happy to go with the flow.

   1   2   3   4   5   6   7   8   9   10

10. I am very conscious of my impact on the environment and place a high priority on recycling and conservation.

   1   2   3   4   5   6   7   8   9   10

Next total the scores for each question to create a number out of a hundred. The closer your total is to a hundred, the more in touch with your feminine side you are. Remember, there is no right or wrong response, and these questions are simply a gauge to get you thinking about the extent of your own femininity.

Chapter 5

Providing the Food: Exploring Masculine Energy

The priority of the masculine, in men and
women, is the mission which leads to freedom.

—David Deida

Hunting for food now commonly takes place from the living room sofa, with the game console in hand and big screen television at the ready. Pursuing, fighting, adventure-based games with a do-or-die or a win-or-lose theme litter the gaming shelves of modern-day shopping malls. Hunting is now more of a hobby or sport as opposed to a way of life. Regardless of the modern-day way this activity takes place, whether it's on the screen or part of a weekend ritual with friends, all approaches seek to provide an artificial filler to meet a man's core needs. The reality is the food on the kitchen table is now purchased at the local supermarket and the act of hunting to provide takes on a very different meaning in the twenty-first century.

Society has evolved. Things have changed. Yet at a fundamental level there are still core needs of the masculine and feminine energy that must be met, and it's fascinating to reflect on the ways in which we seek to meet these needs from an entirely new playing field. And in the same breath it is equally as fascinating to note the way in which these same needs become repressed when suitable outlets are not identified for meeting our core needs in our modern-day world.

As a generalisation, the primary mode of expression for men is masculinity. At his core nature a man feels much more pleasure when his masculine essence is in full force. With the previous chapter focusing on feminine energy as the natural state for females, this chapter now focuses on the expression of masculine energy specific to males, exploring relevant impacts in a relationship context.

**At his core nature a man feels much more pleasure
when his masculine essence is in full force.**

It's interesting that this chapter was actually the last piece I wrote for this book despite its placement as chapter 5 of nine chapters. I worked around the gap in the manuscript until the point where this was the only section left to fill. While the content of this book serves people from all walks of life, the copy was originally developed in response to challenges presented by women aged twenty-five to forty-five years. My focus was therefore on ensuring the context of this chapter on masculine energy was put together to best serve this target audience while it accurately reflected the needs of men in society today in the context of being written from a woman's perspective. This took me sometime before I felt I had the right balance of detail, and I thank all the men in my life who assisted me in ensuring I gave this chapter the further consideration I felt it required.

The chapter begins by exploring masculinity in a changing environment and then goes on to look further at males and masculine energy and why women test their men. Regardless of your sex, I would encourage you to take interest and open your mind to the insights that follow, remembering that both masculine and feminine energy exists within all of us. In the same breath our mates are our mirrors, and without contrast, we cannot truly know who we are. It's all relevant.

Masculinity in a Changing Environment

Many males in society today are confused and lack direction about what it means to connect with the true nature of their masculinity. Emasculation is rife, and granted, though we are no longer out hunting for our food, the need for strong, masculine men remains necessary and essential for men living fulfilling lives.

As part of the discussion of masculinity it is essential to reflect on our changing environment. What does it mean to be a man, and how is manliness or masculinity defined in today's world? And more importantly, do our definitions of manliness allow the core needs of men to be met in a meaningful way?

When we are reflecting on our changing environment, of particular focus is the series of significant social changes that began around the 1900s and accelerated following World War II. Firstly the transition from an agrarian to an industrial economy in the early 1900s and the movement of families from rural areas to urban areas had a profound social impact for men and their sons. The shift to a manufacturing society and urban migration meant boys were separated from their fathers and other male role models. In an agrarian society boys connected with their fathers through working alongside them in the fields and on the maintenance of the family land. Boys learnt how to be men by watching their fathers at work just as their fathers had learnt from their own fathers. Sons mirrored their fathers in their quest to connect with masculinity. Trials of testing the boundaries and learning the limits were done in a generally safe environment where fathers were available as role models.

Following World War II, as families migrated from rural areas to urban locations for work, the contact between fathers and their sons diminished significantly. Dads began to leave home each day to go to work the nine-to-five (though often longer), working-class routine. With the unavailability of dads during this time, mothers were required to step up and take on the role of both parents. This saw women taking on a more masculine role in the home, and in the absence of fathers it encouraged a disconnection from the feminine to support the family, as explored in the previous chapter. With this disconnect from her natural feminine state, stress, exhaustion, and resentment were common by-products for females during this era. The truth is even the most well-intended mothers are not equipped to teach their sons how to be men. With the introduction of the Industrial Revolution, we see a profound change in social dynamics that arguably contributed to states of disconnect and confusion for both men and women. The introduction of the modern-day education system also coincided with the birth of the Industrial Revolution. While dads were at work, sons were being raised by their mothers and then educated in a female-dominated schooling system. In this space masculinity for men became defined by and dependent on the approval of women. As a result, many modern-day men have adopted a female perspective of masculinity based on pleasing the core needs of females. When a man's energy is focused on pleasing females, he buys into the belief that it's actually not okay to just be who he is, and he becomes disconnected from his own sense of purpose.

In addition to these social dynamics, radical feminism in the 60s and 70s further attacked a man's sense of self. As we've touched on previously in chapter 1 and chapter 4, the rise of feminism had a major impact on the balance of masculine and feminine energy for both men and women. This included the rise of a social climate that convinced women they could live alone and that a man was not necessary. Vocal feminists claimed that men were an unnecessary nuisance and promoted women as people who were able to take on the world solo. More than likely the majority of women during this era did not feel this way, yet enough angry voices collaborated to impact the overall social climate and attitude towards men. Men who were already conditioned to look to women for approval were particularly impacted by this harsh social belief. More and more men were struggling to figure out what women wanted and were striving to meet these expectations in order to be loved. Men were positioned to hide their flaws and become what others, especially women, wanted them to be.

Of course, all of these points need to be considered in context. In chapter 1 and chapter 4 we have already touched on the three waves of feminism, the push for equality, and the social impact for females in a changing environment. I'm not arguing that any of these social movements were right or wrong. Rather, my intention in exploring these topics is to prompt further consideration at your end on specific cultural movements throughout history and their impact on our world today. Perhaps you've witnessed behaviours from your parents or your parent's parents that are clearly a result of their historical conditioning. The modern-day atmosphere for which our current relationships exist did not simply appear from a vacuum.

Males and Masculine Energy

A man's primary fuel for growth and fulfillment in life is connection with his life's mission and purpose. His mission is his priority, and unless he knows and is connected to his mission, his core will feel empty. He needs connection with his purpose in order to feel competent, and success and achievement are foremost in his life. Of course, the meaning of success and achievement will be different for each man based on his map of the world, yet at the heart of his meaning will rest the certainty of knowing he is needed.

In a relationship context this core need of the masculine can become a sticking point if it is not appropriately acknowledged and supported. In the previous chapter we explored the primary needs of the feminine as the love and flow of relationships, where her relationship with her significant other is of highest value. Yet here in the space of the masculine, his life purpose must come before the relationship to be true to his core. While the search for love is the priority of the feminine, the mission or the search for freedom is the priority of the masculine. This is not to say that a relationship is not of a high value—and relationships may be connected to his life purpose—just that this is not always the case. Rather, a smooth-functioning relationship is what supports a man to be the best version of himself and to focus on his life purpose. Make a list of the ten most powerful men in society, particularly those who you perceive to be in alignment with their mission and purpose. Next notice if they have strong women or families to support them, and it is highly likely they do. Even prominent men who experience divorce or relationship break-ups will often quickly welcome another female into their lives to fill the void, often remarrying easily and effortlessly. Yet while filling the void with a female presence is important, his mission and purpose remains his primary focus.

In his work *The Way of the Superior Man,* David Deida states,

> Every man knows that his highest purpose in life
> cannot be reduced to any particular relationship. If
> a man prioritises his relationship over his highest
> purpose, he weakens himself, disserves the universe,
> and cheats his woman of an authentic man who can
> offer her full, undivided presence.

**While the search for love is the priority of
the feminine, the mission and search for
freedom is the priority of the masculine.**

In his work *Think and Grow Rich,* Napoleon Hill explains how love, romance, and sex are all emotions capable of motivating men to heights of superior achievement. The desire for sexual expression is the strongest and most impelling of all human emotions. Napoleon Hill states, "For this very reason this desire, when *harnessed and transmuted* into action, other than that of physical expression, may raise one to the status of a genius." Sex energy has an incredible ability to propel men in the direction of their mission and purpose. A teacher who trained and directed the efforts of more than thirty thousand salespeople made the discovery that highly sexed men are the most efficient salesmen. Their sex energy is communicated through the magnetism of their handshakes, the tones of their voices, their postures, the way they carry their bodies, and the vibrations of their thoughts. Hill concludes, "Master salesmen attain the status of master in selling, because they, either consciously, or unconsciously, transmute the energy of sex into sales enthusiasm." Within a similar theme, Hill writes that one of America's most successful businessmen openly admitted that his incredibly attractive secretary was responsible for most of his business ideas and plans. He admitted that her presence lifted him to heights of creative imagination and motivation, such as he could experience under no other stimulus. Again here we see the link between the power of feminine presence and the direct impact on a man's mission and purpose.

A closer look at the structure of male and female brains can provide further insights as to why males tend to be more physical and females tend to be more emotional. To begin, the male brain is ten times larger than the female brain, and the part of the brain associated with sexual desire, aggression, and other physical pleasures—the preoptic section of the hypothalamus—is 2.2 times larger than that in females. This area of the brain is involved in mating behaviour and demonstrates how a man's urges for sexual relations and other physical desires are usually more pressing than they are in women. Men and masculine energy tend to be focused on action, direction, and goal-orientated outcomes. When flipped from physical to emotional, the male brain has a smaller limbic system than women's. The limbic system is primarily responsible for our emotional lives and our abilities to bond and connect with others. This area of the brain also has a great deal to do with the formation of memories and demonstrates why females often communicate using feelings and can pick up on emotional cues that men may be oblivious to.

In summary, females tend to be strong at communication, connection, emotional sensitivity, and nurturing, while males tend to be stronger at logical thinking, problem solving, and physical tasks. Acknowledging these differences creates increased respect for the opposite sex and reinforces the point that we are not the same and that our differences should be celebrated.

To further build on these insights from the structure of the brain, there are several basic needs that we can explore in more depth to begin to understand more about males and masculine energy. These primary masculine needs include respect, sex, adventure, nourishment, and rest. Of course, there are other needs and desires of individual personalities, yet these foundational needs give us a strong understanding of the key desires of the masculine.

To begin, respect and appreciation are core needs of the masculine. For men, their work is very important to them, and many associate what they do for a living with their self-worth. Men also measure their success based on what they can provide or offer a woman, and again this links directly to self-worth. Men have a yearning to figure out their place in the world and to make sense of their surroundings through a career, hobby, or sport that makes them feel respected. At its core it's the hunter-provider mentality that continues to fuel the innate needs of the masculine even in our modern-day world. While the prey is no longer caught with bow and arrow out in the fields, the concept remains the same. Men need to feel like what they do on a daily basis is bringing home the meat (e.g., providing the food) as part of the *Love on the Kitchen Table* model. In today's society the prey takes on a very different form, and women are often equally as good at catching the prey and sometimes better. Many women today make more money than their spouses, and they are often independent, better educated, and totally self-sufficient. While this achievement of equality and access to these areas of success is an important milestone to be celebrated for women, the impact on males and their masculinity must also be considered.

※

Respect and appreciation are core
needs of the masculine.

※

When it comes to men, the bottom line is that women need to offer them respect and appreciation for all the ways in which a man does his job well. It is essential that men find both solace and support in a relationship that continues to validate and show respect for what they do. The key words that men need to hear are "I'm so proud of you" or "I appreciate you," and these signs of appreciation must be regular to support the masculine desire to find a place where they can be free from criticism and be totally accepted and respected. This is how men with their dominant masculine energy experience love. For males reading this insight, may it provide you the freedom to seek that which you crave. For females, may you appreciate the differences in the core needs of males and females and share with your man your appreciation and respect.

In addition to the emotional need to feel appreciated, the physical needs of men are equally as important. We explored how the male brain has a larger preoptic area of the hypothalamus, and it is this area that controls sexual aggression and mating behaviour. We also explored sex as a core need of the masculine, and we know men have both biological and biochemical responses that cause them to crave physical intimacy. Sexual transmutation also assists with a man's motivation and action towards his mission and purpose. In her work *The Secret of the Masculine and Feminine Energies,* Tanya Copprue writes, "Take sex away from a man and you will physically, psychologically and even emotionally destroy him." She goes on to illustrate a study on why men cheat and says the number one answer when it came to sexual dissatisfaction was "sex with my wife was generally too infrequent." This represented 48 per cent of men in the study and reinforces the importance of physical love for meeting the needs of the masculine. Issues can arise when women feel that a man's strong focus on sexual needs demonstrates a lack of interest in the emotional elements of the relationship. Most often this is not actually the case, and thinking along these lines simply shows a lack of understanding and respect for how males and females think. Sex is one of the most spiritual and powerful forces of energy on earth, and it is the very action that creates life. Having a high sexual nature awakens power and fosters a healthy and solid bond between men and women who love one another. We must be grateful for the strong connection with the masculine energy that enforces and drives this physical bond. A masculine focus on sex is a true gift.

The larger preoptic area of the hypothalamus also controls a man's desire for physical activity and aggression that, when combined with a testosterone-filled body, makes for a strong yearning of physical action, adventure, and play. Men must have a way to release this energy and are often attracted to participating in or watching a high level of competitive adventure and sporting activities. This may include sports, such as rugby, league, soccer, hockey, basketball, martial arts, wrestling, running, hiking, cycling, competition fishing, or car racing, basically anything with a competitive nature. From a young age, these types of activities combined with the hustle and bustle of boyhood work to develop young boys into men. The rough-and-tumble nature of many of these physical activities often comes with a man-up approach to getting through and achieving success. These competitive sports also create an atmosphere for male bonding as part of their natural ritual, and for all of these reasons competitive sports are essential channels for men to connect with their sense of masculinity.

Next, based on the fact that men are more physically aggressive than women and expend a lot more energy, it is no surprise that good food and sufficient rest are additional core needs of strong masculine men. The hypothalamus area of the male brain, the area that controls hunger and thirst, is larger in men and has more cells than women. This scientific structure of the way men function drives their strong appetites, and often men will eat almost anything. I can recall my grandma teaching me in my younger years that "the way to a man's heart is through his stomach," and in fact, there is a strong truth to this. Given this natural desire to eat high volumes of food, men must be conscious of what types of foods go into their bodies. A diet high in fresh, whole foods will contribute to healthier sperm and stronger overall physical health, supporting the previous core needs of sex and physical activity.

With a strong diet to support physical activity, rest comes hand in hand as a key component and core need for men. In order to achieve the very physical needs of the masculine energy, good rest is essential, and a lack of rest will lead to a lack of physical performance.

It's amazing that when you deliver love in a way your partner prefers to receive it, you move from a self-centred approach to love to an other-centred way of loving—one that truly respects your partner's experience of life. Women and men need different things, and they experience love in different ways. If you continually strive for an equal playing field in the sense of sameness, you risk opening the doorway for external conflict, and you deprive yourself of a true and deep connection with yourself and your significant other.

Why Women Test Their Men

Most arguments are not really about whether the toilet seat is up or down or who took out the trash. These are simply surface issues. Instead, it's a deeper, more fundamental issue that fuels these superficial conflicts. The secret is to uncover the hidden meaning and to zoom out to reflect on what is *actually* going on. You must understand the bottom-line difference that is causing the conflict and be open to drawing on that sense of respect for the way in which your lover experiences life. To put this is context; let's take a closer look at why women *really* test their men.

The testing phase is fundamentally related to the core need of the female and feminine energy. She will test her man continuously until she can know for sure that she can trust him to hold his ground and be there for her no matter what. Even when she reaches a perceived level of trust, she will still check in with a small test every now and then to ensure he remains strong in his ability to keep her safe. In this sense, while the levels of testing may reduce significantly over time, the core need and act of testing is continuously at play in the context of a relationship and is therefore a fundamental concept to understand.

**A woman will test her man continuously
until she can know for sure that she
can trust him to hold his ground and
be there for her no matter what.**

As part of this testing cycle, you will see small-scale arguments escalating rapidly to full-steam, break-up-material fights. You'll recognise arguments that begin with "why didn't you take out the trash?" and end with her saying, "That's it. We're over." The argument gets so out of hand that it's challenging to recognise what the initial trigger was in the first place. She feels like a complete emotional psychopath, and he interprets the whole thing on a logical level with comments like this: "It's just the garbage. It's not such a big deal." These two extremes of interpretation then tend to escalate the situation even further. In the midst of the argument emotions are high, yet when you zoom out to reflect on what is really happening, new elements of the situation become visible. At the core of the issue she is testing her man to know that she is safe and protected. When he fails to come through for her, the generalisations begin. "I have to do *everything* myself." "You *never/always*—" The stressful feeling of having to do *everything* herself is an example of feeling like she is overcompensating in the masculine space. What she really means is that she needs her man to step up and take action. When she walks out of the room and slams the door, he must follow. Her action of leaving the room tests the nature of his response. Through her actions what she is really saying is this: "Does he have my back, and will he be here for me no matter what?" This is the underlying question being asked throughout this interaction.

As I've mentioned, it's never really about the trash. It's never about the towel on the floor or the fact that the toilet seat's lid was left up. These are just the metaphors for the sabre-toothed tiger. If he can't come through for her on these smaller items, how will he respond when the real danger arrives and she needs him to meet her core need for safety and protection. It's innate.

It's human. And it's real. The testing is the preparation for when the real crisis arrives. The message is this: "I love you, but I need to know I can trust you." If he can come through for her on these smaller things, then she'll trust him to be her man. But if he can't, then he becomes her child, and the dissatisfaction sets in. When she is left to operate at high levels in the masculine state and *do* everything herself, this is when stressful feelings and frustration begin. From here simple disagreements can quickly escalate.

So here's the key: When she throws things, he must love her anyway. Flying crockery really translates to this: "Can you take it?" When she yells and screams in an unfair and unreasonable way, again what she is really saying is this: "Can you take it?" And the response she is looking for is that he can take it and can handle so much more than what she can attempt. She needs to hear him say, "Is that all you've got? There is nothing you can say or do. I love you completely. I can take this, and I'm not going anywhere. Tell me more about what's going on for you right now." He must stand his ground, gently cup her face in his hands, and assure her that he is there for her no matter what. This is what the argument about putting out the trash is really about. She is testing him and asking, "Can I trust and depend on you?" It's what every woman needs to be sure of. For any woman reading this who is resisting the idea, you have already taught yourself that no man will ever pass your test. Lads, it's time to grab a pen. The next time your woman tests you, your role is to step up and gain her trust. Remind her that she is safe, loved, and protected and that you will be there for her always. If she runs, you follow and prove to her that you are there for her no matter what. If she slams the door, you break through it. If she cries and hides her head under the pillow while she is screaming at you to go away, you stay. It's the test. Will you take the easy way out and leave as she requests, or will you lift the pillow, gently embrace her face in your hands, and remind her of who you are? She is looking for strength, confidence, her rock, and her protector. In this space she can melt. In this space she can forgive. In this space she can connect with the power of vulnerability and return to focus on her feminine, to *be* the woman she desires to be.

In the beginning of a relationship it is likely she will test her man more often, and the more he fails her tests, the more she will increase the intensity and frequency of the tests. If he continues to fail the tests, one of two things will happen. Either the quality of the relationship will quickly decline to a point where neither partner is satisfied anymore, resulting in the breakdown of the partnership, or she will choose to settle for mediocrity. On an unconscious level she loses trust in her man and his ability to step up, and in this space she may choose to take on more masculine energy as she sets out to fill this void. It is here where we often see women losing touch with their femininity and adopting strong exteriors. When she moves towards a more masculine state, the power and true beauty of the complementary opposites of masculine and feminine energy in their natural states can never truly be realised. What we begin to see in the relationship is a strong, overpowering woman matched with an emasculated man. While the relationship may still continue to function, the levels of contentment are likely to be much lower.

These insights are incredibly powerful because when you learn to respect, understand, and cater to the core needs of your loved one, then you can ensure he or she is receiving love in the way that most resonates with that person. What often happens in a relationship is that you tend to give love in the way you know you prefer to receive it. In this sense, women will often look to care for their men in the same way they desire to be cared for. Men will likely strive to say thanks for the work their partners do just as they like to be appreciated. Yet at the heart of this mismatched communication the core needs of both are not being fully realised. This doesn't mean that men don't appreciate being cared for and that women don't appreciate a thank-you. That's not it at all. Rather, the message is in relation to the deeper core needs that exist. While these surface examples of respect and love are great, it is also essential that you are meeting the more fundamental needs of your loved one.

**You must give love in the way that
your loved one best receives it.**

Imagine we all have a love tank that just like a petrol tank keeps us fueled with loving emotion. Dr. Gary Chapman speaks of this concept in his work *The Five Love Languages*. Each time you experience love, your tank gets filled. In the same sense, if you do not experience love, then your tank becomes empty, leading to dissatisfaction and eventually the breakdown of the relationship. The less targeted compliments and acts of love are like filling the tank one tenth at a time as opposed to the more targeted acts of love that meet the core needs of each person directly and fill the tank much more quickly.

Women test their men when their love tanks are low, when they are feeling stressed, or when they require reassurance that their core needs can be met as part of the relationship. It's not a game, and it's not about setting him up to fail. She wants him to succeed. She *needs* him to succeed. And when he does, she will appreciate him more than ever before.

Chapter Summary

This chapter's focus on masculine energy along with the previous chapter's focus on feminine energy works in harmony to provide you with insights on the polarity of love. These polarities are special and unique and should be cherished for the gifts that exist within each. One cannot be recognised without the other, and when the core needs associated with each are suppressed, disharmony arises and impacts our ability to experience love. Men with a preferred masculine essence but who seek to fit in with the feminine style of cooperation and flow do themselves a huge injustice. As they unconsciously suppress the masculine, disconnection with their true purpose and life mission diminishes to a frustrating state of hopelessness. In the same breath females with true feminine essences can experience stress and other manifested illnesses following prolonged periods of being plugged in to an excess of masculine energy. Year after year operating to fit in with the masculine style of our working world can lead to disconnection with the feminine. Ultimately suppressing your preferred essence into a falsely balanced persona affects virtually every part of your life, particularly your relationship with your significant other.

When core needs are denied, you deprive yourself of the possibility of true and real love. Instead you must be grounded in mutual respect and equality. In this space you must support and celebrate the differences of males and females or masculine and feminine energy. A man must have the freedom to discover his life mission and then live it, challenging the edge of what's known and operating with purpose and direction. A woman must then be comfortable in her space of love and flow, acknowledging that her sense of self is intimately entwined with the quality of her relationships. Both approaches are unique and must be understood for the intimate sense of fulfillment they bring about.

This book could not exist with reference to one without the other. Chapter 6 explores the celebration of differences further.

Exercises for Reflection

Following your reflection on masculine energy throughout this chapter, explore the following questions to further embed your learning and the relevance to your own world right now.

1. If you think of your energy like a pie graph, what percentage of feminine versus masculine traits do you feel you portray in your life right now?

2. What specific evidence tells you that this balance is true?

3. How does this balance play out in your relationship right now?

4. While you were exploring this chapter, what specific things have you identified that you would like to change to assist you in reaching your relationship goals?

5. What has been the biggest gift in reading this chapter for you personally?

Take the Quiz: How Masculine Are You?

The below questions are designed to get you thinking about the nature of masculinity and to gauge your own current connection with the masculine. Respond to each of the questions based on the level at which you feel you relate to the statement, where one equals "I don't relate at all" and ten equals "I completely relate to this statement."

1. I am confident making decisions, and I make decisions often, always prepared to back myself and stand by my thoughts.

   1   2   3   4   5   6   7   8   9   10

2. I am connected with my mission and purpose in life and actively strive to achieve results in this area.

   1   2   3   4   5   6   7   8   9   10

3. I am comfortable in the role of a leader.

   1   2   3   4   5   6   7   8   9   10

4. I have a sense of pride when it comes to the protection and provision for my family.

   1   2   3   4   5   6   7   8   9   10

5. I put boundaries in place and am comfortable holding the line.

   1   2   3   4   5   6   7   8   9   10

6. I am not afraid to work through conflict.

   1   2   3   4   5   6   7   8   9   10

7. I take responsibility for meeting my own needs.

   1   2   3   4   5   6   7   8   9   10

8. I am clear and direct with my communication.

   1   2   3   4   5   6   7   8   9   10

9. I am comfortable in my own skin and operate with an internal air of confidence.

   1   2   3   4   5   6   7   8   9   10

10. I am a strong role model and leader in the areas I am most passionate about.

    1   2   3   4   5   6   7   8   9   10

Next total the scores for each question to create a number out of a hundred. The closer your total is to a hundred, the more in touch with your masculine side you are. Remember, there is no right or wrong response, and these questions are simply a gauge to get you thinking about the extent of your own masculinity.

Chapter 6

Saying Grace: The Power of Gratitude

You have a gift of 86,400 seconds today.
Have you used one of them to say thank you?
—William Arthur Ward

The train is overcrowded as the businessman reflects on his daily tasks ahead. Smartphones are amazing devices, yet their ability to transform the train seat into an office desk blurs the limits of the working day. At least he has a seat. Concentration on the task at hand is challenging. A few rows ahead of him on the opposite side of the aisle, three children are running a riot. One is swinging from a hand strap attached to the roof while the other attempts to pull him down by his pants. Loud laughter mixed with quick moments of conflict echo through the air accompanied by the occasional shriek as both children fight to gain access to the swinging strap. There are a few kicks and bumps to nearby passengers, and judgements grow heavy. The third child sits in the seat by what appears to be their father. Loud sounds of firing guns echo from his game console and add to the commotion. No one is impressed. Of her own accord, an older lady asks the children to calm down and be a little quieter. Silence is achieved for a mere thirty seconds before the children slip back in to action.

The businessman's increasing frustration at the noise is giving him a headache. Those around him are equally irritated by the interruption to their daily commute. How can the father be allowing such disruptive behaviour? He seems immune to it all and simply sits quietly, staring straight ahead. *Obviously a lack of parenting skills*, thinks the businessman.

Thirty tiring minutes later during his transition stop from platform five, the businessman turns to find himself standing right next to the father of the three restless children. They're not far away, continuing with their antics. A little intrigued at the man's blasé approach to parenting, he prompts polite conversation regarding the weather. Slightly surprised, the businessman discovers the father is incredibly well mannered and seems like a reasonable guy. As the discussion progresses, the businessman learns of the events of the father's morning. It turns out his wife is incredibly unwell in the hospital, and they have received news of a terminal illness. They are actually returning from the hospital now. The father confides that his children are playing up like he's never seen before, yet he feels he needs to give them time to understand what's going on in whatever way they require.

"Perhaps they are still in shock," he says, bowing his head again in reflection.

Often you can judge others much too quickly without knowing the full extent of their circumstances. An arrogant father becomes a mere victim in only a few seconds. Naughty children become lost souls. Judging passengers become overcritical and unreasonable in their thoughts. New information brings new meaning. Yet the event remains the same. In every moment of every day you are choosing the meaning you give to the world around you based on your own perception of reality. In this space events and daily experiences are open to any interpretation, and no one meaning assigned by an individual can be exactly the same as the next. This is the beauty of individuality. With the same stroke of beauty, discord can arise when you don't acknowledge or respect the uniqueness of one world to the next. The secret to truly experiencing a deep state of understanding is to first respect other people's views of the world, knowing their views are based on their individual map of what they know to be true. Secondly you must respect their thoughts and choose to come from a space of gratitude where you can acknowledge and appreciate the learning's that you personally experience as part of every unique interaction.

**In every moment you are choosing the meaning
you give to your world.**

This theme of respect and gratitude is the heart of this chapter and an essential element of the *Love on the Kitchen Table* model. Key themes explored in this chapter include the following: adopting an attitude of gratitude, the importance of celebrating the differences between males and females, respecting the map of others to create a connection based on mutual trust and understanding, and exploring your partner's love map. These insights are ideal for understanding how best to integrate the balance of masculine and feminine energy, as explored in the previous two chapters, in a way that best supports your relationship.

Adopting an Attitude of Gratitude

As a brief historical snapshot, the practice of saying grace entered into the English language through Judeo-Christian cultures and the Jewish mealtime prayer Birkat Hamazon. Birkat Hamazon was a prayer said after meals, and it required taking the time out to pause and be grateful for the meal. This practice has been molded over the years and perpetuated by family traditions and social institutions. The Oxford Dictionary details a broad definition of grace as the name for any number of short prayers or speeches of thanks said before or after a meal. Saying grace specifically thanks either God, whatever that may mean to an individual, and/or any number of entities that have given of themselves to bring the meal to those partaking. This reciting of thanks prior to eating is traditionally referred to as "saying grace" and is a symbol of respect and gratitude. It is also a powerful metaphor when it comes to creating relationship success because just as we should be grateful for the food on our table, we should be equally grateful for all other elements of our world, including the company with which we share our meal. Making shifts in the way you view your relationship can take place immediately, which is what makes this such a powerful insight for linking the concepts of this book.

From what I've observed, the people in the world who are the most fulfilled and who achieve the most are the ones who pause and take the time to have daily gratitude for the small things in life. They consistently appreciate what they have during both times of success and during times of adversity. They are level in their thinking as opposed to having extreme emotional highs followed by extreme emotional lows. Instead their balanced approach acknowledges the bad with the good, the challenges with the successes, and the chaos with the fruition. It's all how you choose to view the situation. Is the glass half empty or half full? Or is it both, and are you willing to be grateful either way? This is the key. Gratitude in *all* situations, whether initially perceived as supportive or challenging, is the secret to lasting fulfillment and to experiencing the depths of love.

In his book *The Gratitude Effect*, human behaviour expert Dr. John Demartini says,

Any moment of our life that we cannot recall with gratitude is a moment that we have not yet fully examined. Had we examined that moment, we would have recognised the magnificent hidden order, that some philosophers and theologians call the secret workings of the divine master plan. In actuality, there is nothing but love.

What would happen if you were to acknowledge love in all interactions within your relationship? What would happen if instead of focusing on the nitpicking, the lack of support, or what you perceive to be missing, you instead chose to focus on the parts of the situation you can be grateful for? This is my challenge to you.

Gratitude in *all* situations is the secret to experiencing the depths of love.

To live with an attitude of gratitude is one of the most powerful and spiritual states you can choose. People who count their blessings and are grateful for their lives receive more to be grateful for. I once heard Dr. Demartini describe gratitude as the key that opens up the gateway of the human heart, where inside the heart is amazing inspiration and a tremendous amount of human love. When you choose to start each day with gratitude and choose to end each day with gratitude, thankfulness, and grace, your day unfolds on levels that you may previously not have had the chance to experience. When you have your heart open with gratitude, your greatest potential is unveiled, and things must play out differently based on your thinking.

Celebrating Differences

As I write this section I have Aretha Franklin's hit song "Respect" playing through my mind. It comes complete with some impressive booty-shaking and a feeling of complete confidence radiating from within. While Franklin's cover is often attributed as a landmark for the feminist movement, my interpretation speaks of a more global respect and in this case one that specifically focuses on the beauty of both men and woman. It's the perfect soundtrack for this chapter, and I encourage you to complement your own reading with some background music of your choice. Select tunes that symbolise what respect means to you because these are the key themes that so perfectly weave the learning surrounding masculine and feminine energy together in an atmosphere of love and appreciation.

In this space of appreciation and gratitude, as part of "saying grace," it is time to celebrate the differences between men and women. When you can release your need to reach a level of sameness, then you can begin to truly experience the magic in bringing the two unique energies together. To further put this into context, we can explore anthropological evidence that suggests we evolved from hominids whose lives were mapped by very gender-specific roles. Females specialised in nurturing young while males focused on cooperative hunting. As nursing mothers, the amount of milk produced from the body is affected by how relaxed you feel, which is related to the release of the hormone oxytocin in the brain. Natural selection would therefore favor those females who were able to calm down quickly after they felt stressed in order to produce milk easily and effortlessly, optimising the chance of survival for the young.

At the other end of the scale, natural selection would reward the opposite energy for males in their role as cooperative hunters. In this activity maintaining attentiveness was a key survival skill. So males whose adrenalin kicked in quickly and who did not calm down so easily were more likely to survive and therefore procreate.

When you take these initial observations on their own, you can already begin to see how the difference in males and females is directly related to natural states and roles. Instead of denying these differences or working towards a sense of sameness, we must celebrate the different roles for the innate strengths that make them so special and unique.

This evidence of differences should be celebrated, yet all too often I hear examples of men and women putting their spouses down, tapping into common language and beliefs that exist within society. For the ladies, coffee time catch-ups can be littered with references such as the following: "Ah, men, they're all the same . . . useless." "If only women ruled the world—". You will most likely recognise statements of similar themes. Whether you are guilty of sharing these types of words and phrases yourself or you recognise them as the words from friends, colleagues, or daily media, the essential thing to note is the tone and underlying messaging that you are feeding your unconscious mind when you are engaging in or listening to messages along these lines.

Women of the twenty-first century often get stuck in thinking that men should be more like them instead of honoring their masculine gifts. In this state men become emasculated within society. In addition, as a woman with this perception, you will never truly be able to experience what it means to embrace a real man in your life if you do not allow the space for him to exist. Men have many gifts to share with the world. They protect and provide. They lead with direction and a strong sense of focus, and they bring a light-hearted sense of adventure to life. Many men are also great at fixing things. Yet most importantly their dominant masculinity is what allows females to embrace their natural state of femininity. This is the ultimate gift above all else.

Too many men are also guilty of adopting unresourceful language and terms of reference for referring to their loved ones. References to "the missus" or "old bag" are far too common. I'm being polite with the examples I am sharing. I actually find this section hard to write and the language in which many refer to the opposite sex challenging to understand and shocking to accept. No wonder we have a world full of conflict in relationships when we have access to such a wide range of insulting language. You only need to switch on an episode of long-standing sitcom *Two and a Half Men* to witness the array of mainstream sexist jokes that exist in society today. When you allow these messages into your world, they get filed away in the unconscious mind as associations to what it means to be a man or woman. While you may not repeat the messages word for word, your associations become shrouded in an environment that is not conducive to your relationship success.

Instead Aretha Franklin's "Respect" must replace judgement. You must allow a space of kindness and acceptance when it comes to acknowledging differences between men and woman, and these differences must be celebrated. In this space you can begin to understand that the core needs are unique for both men and women based on the natural, complementary balance of masculine and feminine energy.

When you understand this, you can then frame your communication in a way that best respects the map of your loved one. For example, to feel alive in his masculine form, the male energy must feel connected with his life's purpose and be heading in that direction with focus and determination. His life is about being productive and contributing through doing. The core need for males and the masculine energy is the desire to feel appreciated. Ladies, here's what your man needs to hear on a regular basis: "I really appreciate you." "I really appreciate how you—" "I'm so proud of you." Watch as he takes on this masculine boost of energy and his shoulders pull back and his chest puffs out. He feels proud and worthy. He feels needed, and this fuels his sense of purpose and direction. In this space he is also able to step up even further into his innate role of protector and provider. So when you put your book down and choose to finish reading for today, the very next thing you must do is tell your man how much you appreciate him and for what specifically. If you do not appreciate his masculine essence, it will literally diminish in your presence, and you will be left wondering where all the good men have gone. Masculine men want to be appreciated for what they are doing and where they are going. Appreciation towards your man truly will make the biggest difference in your relationship right now, allowing him to step up even more into his masculine space and for you to then embrace your feminine essence.

The core need of the female or feminine energy is of course very different. Think about it, ladies. When a man says to you, "I'm so proud of you," it's kind of like him saying, "Hmm, that's nice, dear." However, it's a little bit like water off a duck's back. But if he says to you, "I love you, and I want you to know that I will be here for you always no matter what, looking out for you and keeping you safe and protected," then it becomes melt-in-his-arms material. The female or feminine energy needs to be able to trust her man to keep her safe and protected always. She needs to know he has her back and that he will step up and hold his ground when required. In this space she is then able to embrace her femininity and be understood for who she is without having to *do* anything. This space of certainty, comfort, and protection is the core need of the feminine.

Respecting the Map of Others

It is said that in every moment we have millions of pieces of information coming at us through our five main senses. The things we see, hear, feel, taste, and smell all assist us in making sense of the world around us. It's impossible for all the millions of pieces of information to be processed at once, so instead we distort, delete, and generalise our experiences at every moment in order to make sense of our world. What this means is that we each experience a different version of reality based on the way in which we process the information we chose to take in. As an individual, your filtering system allows in whatever you identify as relevant, and everything else becomes deleted, distorted, and generalised. In this sense, you get what you are looking for based on your ideas, attitudes, and beliefs about your world around you.

The way in which you see the world can be referred to as your unique map, which is a mere representation of reality as you choose to focus on it. No one's map is an exact representation of the world just like no geographical map can accurately represent a region. The map is not the territory, and a map of New York is just that—a map. It can never *be* New York. Rather, it is just a representation. Our own maps of the world work in the same way. They are a representation of reality as we individually perceive it.

Two people can interpret the exact same situation in incredibly different ways, depending on their map of the world. While one person interprets a certain expression to mean excitement, another person may be interpreting the exact same expression to mean fear. While a challenging event equals failure for some, it signifies opportunity for others. Is the glass half full or half empty? It's all relative based on your perception of the world.

Your map of the world is a mere representation
of reality as you choose to focus on it.

What happens when you bring two maps of the world together in an intimate connection of love? Under false pretenses we are often lead to believe that two become one, yet in reality *two* individual maps still exist as part of a relationship and must be acknowledged and respected for their distinct features. Challenges arise when you attempt to impose your map of the world on others, and over an extended period of time this imposition can often lead to the breakdown of a relationship. Two dominant egos attempting to control the other are not conducive to relationship success. In his work *The Celestine Prophecy*, James Redfield quotes,

> This one whole person consequently has two heads, or egos. Both people want to run this whole person they have created and so, just as in childhood, both people want to command the other, as if the other were themselves. This kind of illusion of completeness always breaks down into a power struggle. In the end, each persona must take the other for granted and even invalidate them so that they can lead this whole self in the direction they want to go.

You must foster an appreciation and respect for the way in which other people see their worlds. You don't necessarily need to agree with their ways of thinking, but you must respect them in order to have effective communication. You must also understand the difference between love and codependence. In codependency what you can have is one member of the relationship experiencing excessive emotional reliance on the other. In this form, father and mother energy can be unconsciously acted out, allowing the space for little boy or little girl behaviour in the partner who is being nurtured from parent energy. Often this type of relationship is fuelled from a case of not receiving love or support from parents when one was growing up, and therefore, individuals may unconsciously seek that parental love from their spouses. The parent figure is seeking control and fulfilling a gap from childhood while the partner being parented is often seeking the love he or she perceives was lacking while he or she was growing up. The main problem with codependency is that you aren't able to reach your full potential as an individual because of the perceived constraints of your relationship. Alternatively a loving relationship is where two individuals who could live independently alone then come together to share their love and enrich each other's lives.

All messages of communication you receive are constructed from the maps of others and then filtered through your own map. Messages are therefore open for interpretation, and when you can truly acknowledge this point, then you can begin to build greater rapport and foster improved communication. The ultimate forgiveness frame flows naturally from this space. Everyone is doing the best they can with the resources they perceive they have. If they knew how to do better, they would. What would happen if you were to *truly* adopt this belief? And I don't mean read it, memorise it, and say you've got it. I mean truly embrace it in every form of communication going forward as a part of how you operate in your everyday world.

**Everyone is doing the best they can with
the resources they perceive they have.
If they knew how to do better, they would.**

What would really begin to happen if you were to acknowledge other people's maps in all communication, knowing that they are doing the best they can with the resources they perceive they have? How might you approach situations differently? Will you be so quick to judge the man on the train, or will a deeper need to connect allow you to pause, take a moment, and acknowledge this forgiveness frame to open up deep gateways of rapport, connection, and love?

Love Maps: A Solid Foundation for Success

In a relationship context you can take acknowledging the maps of others even further by focusing specifically on love maps. Love maps are the unique maps and sets of perspectives that are brought together as part of a relationship. Marriage therapist and author Dr. John Gottman highlights the importance of love maps as one of his essential guiding principles in his book *The Seven Principles for Making Marriage Work.* He talks of the danger of disconnect when you fall into a habit of inattention to the smaller details of your loved one's life. One of his case studies describes a husband who didn't even know the family dog's name because he spent so much time at work. While this is an extreme case, what it highlights is that the little things matter, and Dr. Gottman stresses the importance of the finer details as the foundation for relationship success. In comparison to inattention to detail, emotionally intelligent couples are intimately acquainted with each other's worlds. "I call this having a richly detailed *love map*— my term for that part of your brain where you store all the relevant information about your partner's life," explains Dr. Gottman. The love map is about knowing the intimate details about your partner, such as his or her favourite colour, his or her preferred winter meal, and the number of scars he or she has on his or her body. It's a relationship based on a deep friendship and a mutual respect for each other's company. Strong couples tend to know each other intimately, and they are well accustomed to each other's likes, dislikes, personality traits, dreams, and aspirations. It's the finer details that build the solid foundation of friendship that supports the relationship. This means when challenges and conflicts arise or the stormy weather sets in, there's a sturdy foundation of support to keep the relationship standing strong during the storm.

Strong couples know each other intimately.

Dr. Gottman talks in his work about a study done by one of his students, Alyson Shaprio. In her study Alyson Shaprio focused on one of the major causes of relationship dissatisfaction and divorce—the birth of a first child. Sixty-seven per cent of couples in her newly-wed study underwent a precipitous drop in marital satisfaction the first time they became parents. The remaining 33 per cent did not experience the same drop, and instead about half of the remaining couples actually quoted an improvement in their relationship.

Alyson's close study of fifty couples found that those couples whose marriages thrived after the birth of their first child had detailed love maps as opposed to the remaining couples who were much more impacted by the new member to the family and consequent upheaval. Ultimately the couples that were already in the habit of keeping up to date with each other's feelings and levels of thinking weren't thrown off course. Instead, with the presence of a new baby in the family, they continued to grow and thrive in their levels of connection. In comparison, those with weaker love maps experienced dramatic shifts resulting from the sudden change in circumstances.

The findings of this study are again reminiscent of chapter 3, where we focused on the core needs of a relationship. While creation and investment in a common area of growth outside of the relationship, such as a child, is essential to a fulfilling relationship, it cannot become the primary focus of the connection. Instead it must be viewed in comparison to the remaining core needs of the relationship—friendship, passionate love, and identity. When all areas are not given equal focus, discord and conflict becomes inevitable.

Time and time again when I am working with clients who are looking to find love after several failed attempts, a common theme they reference as a link to where previous relationships have gone wrong is the point regarding investment in the external. They talk of business ventures, having children, or key external events—such as house renovations or increased care of another family member—as primary events that deterred the focus away from the essence of the relationship itself. From here they talk about "growing apart" or describe how the connection became "weaker," and what they are really referring to is the fact that they lost touch with the details of their significant others' love maps. The finer details of the relationship were not attended to, and when the bigger issues continued to develop or escalate, there was no solid foundation for support. Or as is often the case, there was never a strong foundation there to support them in the first place. Despite differing viewpoints in society, I will continue to stress that the relationship itself *must* be the primary focus of the connection. The child or investment in the external cannot exist without the two parties of the relationship having engaged in the creation in the first place. The best way to father a son is to love his mother. In the same sense, the best way to mother a child is to demonstrate respect for the father and provide a model relationship from which the children can learn their most important foundations for success.

Couples who have worked on creating a solid foundation will be much better placed to weather the storms of life. They have an enduring respect for each other and express this attachment not just in the big ways but also in little ways day in and day out. A detailed love map reinforces friendship as the fuel that ignites the flames of romance.

Chapter Summary

The foundation of the *Love on the Kitchen Table* model is strong; the candles are lit, and the table is set. The two energies, masculine and feminine, have interlaced their strengths to bring the meal to the table and to bring the ambiance alive. Then time must be taken to pause and give thanks and to celebrate the combination of efforts that have made the meal possible. As a metaphor for daily gratitude and appreciation, saying grace is an essential ingredient for embracing a fulfilling relationship. It's about knowing the intimate details about your lover and then truly appreciating him or her for who he or she is. You must strive to understand and appreciate his or her map of the world and get curious to know more about his or her way of thinking. The more you know about each other, the stronger your ties become. Like the foundations of a solid tree, the years of getting to know each other creates a complex system of roots that holds the tree strongly in place regardless of the winds when the storm comes.

Together with a strong respect for your partner's map of the world, an attitude of gratitude allows you the opportunity to experience love at a much deeper level. You are then able to multiply those experiences exponentially to welcome into your life even more of the desired focus. In fact, nothing new can come into your life unless you are grateful for what you already have. Therefore, you must first be grateful for your relationship as it is right now. Begin from this space and make a commitment to say, "Thank you," more often. Tell your loved one how much you appreciate him or her and make random acts of kindness part of your daily lifestyle. In order to experience the true effects of living with an attitude of gratitude, you must actively start to *think* it, to *feel* it, and to *do* it.

Nothing new can come into your life
unless you are grateful for what you already have.

Know your lover. Then appreciate your lover. Simply by shifting your thinking and viewing your relationship from an attitude of gratitude, you can begin to experience levels of love and understanding that previously could not be comprehended.

Let "saying grace" be a theme that ripples throughout the entire essence of your world. Living in an emotional state of gratitude and appreciation will enhance your life more than almost anything else I know of.

Exercises for Reflection

Saying Grace: The Power of Daily Gratitude

This exercise is about introducing the practice of gratitude to your daily routine. When you consciously choose to bring gratitude into your day, you open up the space to discover the true potential of your existence. When you begin and end your day with gratitude, you are celebrating all that is possible as a platform to create even more magic.

Introduce the following practices in to your daily routine:

1. First thing when you wake, choose a time and space to spend a moment connecting with all that you are grateful for.

2. List at least five or more key points that you are grateful for in that moment. You may choose to record these in a paper diary, online, or through an application on your smartphone. Whichever way works for you is fine, providing you are physically recording them in some form to move the points out of your head and into the physical realm.

3. At the end of the day, repeat the process, detailing all that
    you are grateful for in that moment. By the end of each
    day you will have a list of ten or more items for which
    you are grateful. In this space your focus has to change,
    and it already has. Notice how life begins to deliver you
    even more of that which you are grateful for. Because only
    when you are grateful for what you have can the universe
    then begin to deliver you more.

Fifty Questions for Exploring Your Partner's Map of the World

As part of celebrating differences, get curious about your
partner's map of the world. Get comfortable and grab a favourite
beverage, as this next set of exercises is designed to be done
together with your partner so that you can both reflect on your
current knowledge of each other's realities. The below questions
are designed to explore each other's maps.

Universal Relationship Beliefs

1. What does being in a relationship mean to you?
2. What does being a man mean to you?
3. What does being a woman mean to you?
4. What does sex mean to you?
5. What does marriage mean to you?
6. What does family mean to you?
7. What does love mean to you?

8. What do you believe keeps a relationship alive so that it is worth your every breath?

9. What is your biggest relationship fear?

10. What do you think is the ultimate vision for your/our relationship?

Work

11. Are you currently working in your chosen profession?

12. What is your dream job?

13. What does having a job mean to you?

14. Do you consider your work a career or just a job?

15. What is your retirement plan?

Money

16. What does money mean to you? Has this changed over the years, and if so, how specifically?

17. What are your beliefs about earning or having lots of money?

18. How important is it for you to make a lot of money?

19. What are your thoughts on the current state of your finances?

20. How can you step it up even more right now? What one step would make the biggest difference in moving you towards financial freedom?

Your Home

21. If you could live anywhere in the world, where would it be?

22. Do you prefer urban, suburban, or rural lifestyle settings? Have your thoughts on this changed over the years?

23. Is it important for you to own your own home?

24. What role do you believe the kitchen table plays in your home?

25. What do you need to feel inspired and energised in your home?

Leisure and Travel

26. What is your idea of a fun day out?

27. How much money do you regularly spend on leisure activities?

28. Are holidays an important part of your yearly planning?

29. What is your idea of an ideal holiday that you've not experienced yet?

30. Do you think it's important to always have a valid passport?

Social and Events

31. Is it important for you to attend social events regularly, and if so, what type of events? Has this changed over time?

32. What is your ideal date night? How often do you believe you should go on date nights?

33. Which holidays do you believe are the most important to celebrate?

34. Do you maintain a family tradition around certain holidays, or is there a tradition that you'd like to introduce?

35. Do you enjoy receiving gifts?

Sex and Appearance

36. While growing up, what was the attitude toward sex in your family? Was it talked about?

37. Who taught you about sex, and what are your thoughts about how sex is taught in society today?

38. How important is it that you always look your best? Do you have specific routines you embrace on a daily, weekly, or monthly basis?

39. What do you believe about nourishing your body?

40. How much money do you spend on clothing and your appearance each year?

Health

41. What is one lifestyle change you believe would make the biggest difference right now in terms of contributing to your health?

42. Do you believe that taking care of your physical and mental health is a part of honoring your marriage vows?

43. How would you write a description of your own health right now?

44. Who taught you about health, and how have your perceptions changed over the years?

45. In terms of organic, whole foods, how do you think the increased access to these items in our supermarkets is changing the world?

Family and Friends

46. Are you close to your family?

47. How much influence do your parents still have over your decisions? How much influence do friends have in comparison?

48. How did your parents settle conflicts when you were growing up? What did you learn from them?

49. What roles do you believe friends and family plays within a relationship?

50. To what extent are you willing to invest in your relationship with family?

How Well Do You Know Your Partner's Love Map?

Work through the following fifty questions outlined to determine the extent of your knowledge of each other's worlds. For each question you get correct, as deemed correct by your partner of course, mark yourself a point to create a total score of love-map knowledge at the end. Remember, this is not designed as a test to determine something that is right or wrong but instead to provide insights into your current understanding of each other's worlds, knowing that the stronger your love map is for your knowledge of your significant other, the better placed you are to weather the storms of life. Enjoy the questions and approach the exercise with love, respect, and support.

1. What's my favourite colour?
2. What is my favourite wintertime meal?
3. Name my two closest friends (two points).
4. What's my preference, savoury or sweet?
5. What was my first job, and how much did I get paid (two points)?
6. What is my stance on religion?
7. Name my favourite holiday getaway location?
8. What are my top five goals at the moment (five points)?
9. What's my favourite movie?
10. What's my favourite musical instrument?
11. Name three of my primary role models (three points)?
12. Who is my favourite artist?
13. When is my birthday?
14. How much do I weigh?
15. What are my two favourite forms of exercise (two points)?
16. What was I wearing when we first met?
17. What are three challenges I am facing right now (three points)?
18. What turns me on sexually?
19. What time of day do I most prefer to have sex?

20. If I were to receive a random gift of $1,000 today, what would I spend it on?

21. Who is my favourite author?

22. What's my favourite item of clothing right now?

23. Do I prefer urban, suburban, or rural lifestyles?

24. Name three of my favourite hobbies (three points).

25. What was the make and model of my first car I ever owned?

26. What is my mother's middle name?

27. What's my biggest fear?

28. What's my ideal retirement plan?

29. Do I believe in life after death?

30. Who is the family member who has influenced me the most over the years?

31. How many fillings do I have?

32. Name three things that most people *don't* know about me (three points).

33. Do I support a charity, and if not, what charity would I be most likely to support?

34. What's my favourite shopping outlet?

35. What's one of my most embarrassing moments?

36. Am I working in my ideal job, and if not, what is my ideal job?

37. What's my father's birth date?

38. Name two things that make me anxious (two points).

39. What are my three favourite animals (three points)?

40. When was the last time I cried?

41. When was the last time I went to the doctor?

42. Name two birthmarks or scars on my body that not many people know about.

43. What part of your body turns me on the most?

44. What's my least favourite household chore?

45. Which do I prefer, summer or winter?

46. Describe my day today in detail.

47. Name a time in my life I felt the most ripped off.

48. Name three things I'm good at (three points).

49. How do I take my coffee?

50. On what date did we meet?

Add your points to create a total out of seventy. The higher your score, the more detailed your love map of your significant other. Next swap roles and repeat the questionnaire for the other person. Discuss your results. What insights do you notice as you work through these questions?

Chapter 7

Feeding Our Bodies: The Seasons of Intimacy

And when it rains on your parade,
look up rather than down.
For without the rain, there would be no rainbows.

—G. K. Chesterton

The heat was radiating, and their backyard was alive with the buzzing sounds of summer. A young boy of just ten years and his father had found the cocoon of a butterfly. They often spent summer afternoons in the garden, exploring the landscape for new signs of activity. On this particular afternoon, a small opening in the newly sighted cocoon signaled action. They sat and waited eagerly as the butterfly inside began its struggle to force its body through the tiny opening of the cocoon. Several hours passed. The young boy's face grew tired with concern. It appeared as if the butterfly had gotten as far as it could and no further progress seemed to be happening. Finally the father decided to give the butterfly a helping hand. He went inside to retrieve a pair of scissors, and upon his return he winked at the boy to let him know he had a plan. He took the scissors and slowly began to snip off the remaining bit of the cocoon, allowing the butterfly to emerge easily and effortlessly. Yet as the butterfly emerged, it did no more than rest on the ground by the empty cocoon. It had a swollen body and small, shriveled wings. The father and his son continued to watch the butterfly, expecting that at any minute the wings would enlarge and expand so that the insect could support its body and fly to freedom. Neither happened. Instead the butterfly died after only a short while.

You see, what the father and his son did not understand in their kindness and haste was that the restricted opening of the cocoon and the struggle required for the butterfly to get through the tiny opening was nature's way of forcing fluid from the body of the butterfly into the wings. The purpose behind this force of fluid is to prepare the wings for flight once freedom from the cocoon is achieved. Essentially, in playing the role of the rescuer, the father had unknowingly sent the butterfly to its early death.

As part of my work and study of relationships and human behaviour, I've come to realise that all of life has a cycle, and often we must acknowledge each stage of the cycle in order to benefit from the next. There can be no light without darkness, no success without failure, no joy without pain. We must learn to calibrate ourselves through the challenging times to emerge and experience the flight of enjoyment. Disney's 1994 animated film *The Lion King* sums up the concept in its simplest form with the film's theme song "The Circle of Life". It reminds us that all living things have a moment at which they become alive, where the birth marks the first point on the circle of life.

As a broad overview, the circle of life is then characterised by four principal stages:

1. birth
2. growth
3. reproduction
4. death of the physical form

"The Circle of Life" refers to the fact that death is not really the end but the seed of some other life. Albert Einstein indirectly spoke of this concept when he said that energy cannot be created or destroyed, that it merely changes form. In *The Lion King* this concept was demonstrated by the act of the lions eating the antelope. Then once the lions died, the nutrients in their bodies were absorbed into the earth and eventually into the grass, which as part of the cycle was then eaten by the antelope. Everything in existence participates in this great cycle, and within the larger whole, mini cycles exist. I truly believe we are a system of energy, seasons, and cycles that connect us to the greater whole in a pure, spiritual form.

This chapter speaks to this point and specifically explores a series of cycles and their impact on our relationships with our significant others. Many relationship experts use the metaphor of the seasons—winter, spring, summer, and autumn—to describe the key stages of a relationship and to better understand the flow of intimacy. This chapter reflects on these four seasons as symbols for the stages of love and takes the thinking slightly further so that we can look at the mini cycles that exist at an individual level within this set of relationship seasons. This next step in thinking explores the female and male intimacy cycles and their impact on experiencing love.

**We are a system of energy, seasons, and
cycles that connect us to the greater
whole in a pure, spiritual form.**

Once again our kitchen table has the clues for success in each of these areas of focus, where the flow of seasonal food supplies can teach us about human nature. Just as strawberries flourish in the summer months and oranges in the winter, our own feminine and masculine cycles experience times of growth and rest, intimacy and autonomy, love and emptiness. The challenges arise when you begin to manipulate what you perceive to be your preferred state. Often you get caught up in the blueprint of society and create expectations for yourself that require you to experience a continual state of happiness, love, and positivity. Just as society manufactures strawberries and oranges to be available all year round, we tend to expect the same of our own emotions. Yet when you attempt to rescue yourself from what you perceive to be an unresourceful state, you are denying your own true rhythm and flow.

This chapter emphasises how the food on the kitchen table should be influenced by the seasons and natural flow of what the planet is providing during a particular time of year. This seasonal flow is a symbol of rhythm for many areas of life, including the rhythm within our relationships. Just as seasons have certain characteristics, our relationships also experience cycles defined by certain traits and core needs. There is a flow in everything you do, and understanding this flow is incredibly powerful.

This chapter explores the seasons of love as a direct reflection of the planet's seasons of winter, spring, summer, and autumn. It then continues to share insights on intimacy cycles for women and men to further reinforce the importance of acknowledging flow. When you understand these types of cycles, you can then choose to self-regulate your responses and actions towards certain events, creating results more closely aligned with your own personal values and beliefs. By educating you on the different cycles that exist in your relationship, my intention is that you will then be able to identify the patterns playing out in in your current world, affording you the power to make more informed decisions on where you want to be. During the more challenging times in our relationship, Hayden and I have sat down and acknowledged our relationship as experiencing a period of winter—the death of an old chapter making way for the new. This acknowledgement has given us both the space and freedom to just exist in the moment and to go *through* the experience as opposed to fighting it. Understanding the seasons of love and intimacy cycles allows you to normalise and embrace the flow of emotion you experience on a regular basis. Knowledge is power. Rather than tapping in to a continual need for high energy and positivity, you can instead acknowledge and connect with your own emotional flow and that of your surrounding environment, and you can identify resourceful support where required, knowing that all stages of the cycles are normal.

The Seasons of Love

Seasonal shifts occur as part of Mother Nature's nurturing of our planet. With winter comes a time for hibernation, where we battle to protect ourselves from the cooler elements that may include wind, rain, hail, and snow. The trees lose their leaves, and we are left with a barren land. Next comes spring, where the winter cleansing of the landscape has made way for new life. We see the planting of new seeds, the flowering of dormant plants, and the birthing of new energy. Spring then flows through to summer, which is characterised by the maintenance of the crop, the flourishing of the young, and the enjoyment of the warmer climate. As summer flows into autumn, rewards are reaped with continued enjoyment following the efforts of sowing the seeds during spring. Spring, summer, and autumn months then eventually mellow down to the stillness of winter, and again the cycle repeats.

The seasons provide an apt analogy for the changes that occur within relationships. Dr. Gary Chapman defines these seasons in his book *The Four Seasons of Marriage*. He explains that while the analogy of relationship seasons do not necessarily coincide with the timings of the planet's seasons, the symbols work to represent similar themes. Based on Dr. Gary Chapman's work and extended research in this space, I have slightly adapted the themes to create a cycle of hibernation, birthing, growth, and definition. These themes are detailed in this chapter as part of the *Love on the Kitchen Table* model, as the environment for which the table is set. The purpose of this chapter is to help you and your lover identify which area of flow your relationship is currently experiencing. The relationship cycles come and go, and while each one holds the potential for emotional health and happiness, each season as part of the cycle also has associated challenges. The key is to create a solid level of awareness surrounding the seasons and to develop the necessary skills to enhance your relationship and move through the seasonal flows easily and effortlessly.

Winter

Winter is the season of the relationship cycle where elements within the relationship may begin to feel stagnant, still, and flat. During winter it may feel like nothing has really changed for a while. Routine is likely to have led to boredom, a lack of fulfillment, and a disconnect with yourself and your significant other. Love begins to break down. Conversations turn to arguments, and individuals begin to withdraw into silence. There is often a limited sense of togetherness during winter, and couples will often seek third-party support to guide their relationships out of the cooler months of hibernation. Relationship seminars, self-help books, counseling, and coaching can become key tools in assisting the relationship to move forward. In addition, during winter couples must search for new ways of doing things to move forward and get new results. Couples experiencing winter must identify signs of light for the coming season in order to move through this cooler month to discover the early stages of spring. If the couple fails to connect with moving through the renewal phase, then this is where relationships will breakdown, leading to separation.

Characteristics associated with the winter season of a relationship can include the following:

- loneliness
- a lack of communication
- hurtful communication

- frequent arguments

- negativity

- hurt

- anger

- frustration

- disappointment

- hopelessness

- destruction

- discouragement

- emptiness

- critical words

- coldness

While you might recognise some of these characteristics spread sporadically throughout your relationship at times, it is important to note that winter is characterised by a selection of these traits being present for a prolonged period of time to the extent that they have a detrimental impact on the relationship itself. Just as the flowers in our gardens die during the cooler months, the winter stages of a relationship can also be characterised by death or loss. Where there has been no growth or change in a relationship for some time, death and loss become the natural outcomes.

We all experience all seasons of the relationship cycle, and it is important to note that this death and loss season is not necessarily a negative thing and can be experienced in many ways. The loss can be considered as more of a cleansing process where the old way of doing things is cleared out and makes way for the new, more empowering celebrations of love. The flower bed dies, yet the space is cleared for the next garden initiative. The experience of winter therefore rests on a continuum. Some couples may experience the depths of the Alaskan cold, while other couples may simply find themselves in a slight Hawaiian chill.

Where there has been no growth or change in a relationship for some time, death and loss become the natural outcomes.

They key is to acknowledge the winter months as a time of hibernation and reflection within a relationship. A commitment to change will then drive the relationship back into the spring, and partners will experience the relationship on a new level. The need for reflection and a sense of planning for spring is essential during the winter months.

Spring

Spring is the time of dating and courting. Couples in the midst of spring will be experiencing lightness, fun, variety, and a sense of significance surrounding the relationship. It's the falling-in-love stage, and for those who have been together for a long time, it's the falling-in-love-all-over-again stage. Everything becomes new and fresh in the spring with a strong sense of movement towards new beginnings. There is passion and a burning sense of desire. Gratitude and anticipation of the future are the typical attitudes associated with spring. It is often a time for accelerated activities, and couples will do an incredible amount of exciting new things, expressing love and stimulating passion and connection within the relationship.

Characteristics associated with the spring season of a relationship can include the following:

- excitement
- optimism
- gratitude
- a strong sense of togetherness
- appreciation
- hope
- love
- trust
- strong communication
- new beginnings
- a willingness to change and grow
- a commitment to making plans
- a sense of aliveness
- strong nurturing towards the relationship

The central theme is the birthing of love or the rebirthing for those who have been together for a long time. The birthing is internal, and it focuses on nurturing what exists within the relationship, sowing the seeds within your own backyard to deliver what's true for the two of you. It's almost like the outside world disappears with the two of you so intimately entwined in the love that exists for one another.

Spring is where most marriages begin, and the excitement and commitment of creating a new life together enhances the relationship. The depths of winter have cleared the space, and a blank landscape is now available to plant the garden, or relationship in this case, of your ultimate desire. In the case of an early marriage, it is likely that the season of winter has not yet even been experienced, and therefore, the young love of spring is all that is known at the time.

Care must be taken surrounding exactly what is planted during spring. New beginnings, new patterns of life, and new ways of living must have appropriate ecology in order to be sustainable. Ecology in terms of human behaviour refers to the relationship between a person and the environment. It takes into consideration the consequences or impact of a decision on the bigger picture.

Two key questions to ask within your relationship when you are planting the seeds of spring are the following:

1. Is the decision and outcome congruent with other outcomes you have planned to set?

2. Is the outcome or decision compatible with the needs and expectations of your wider environment (family, neighbors, and community)?

If the ecology of a decision is not considered, then you may risk a short and sweet experience of spring followed by an immediate transition to winter. When the ecology of a marriage is not given high consideration, often we see divorce within only two to three years of marriage. Appropriate consideration of ecology and the long-term impacts of your decisions will allow more sustainable seeds to be planted and a prolonged experience of the spring and summer seasons.

Summer

Fun is the theme for summer in a relationship. Life is beautiful. Love is plentiful. During summer you reap the benefits of a well-established spring garden, and your efforts to understand each other and work together as a team begin to pay off.

Characteristics associated with the summer season of a relationship can include the following:

- happiness
- joy
- satisfaction
- contentment

- accomplishment
- connection
- growth
- education
- teamwork
- spirituality
- acceptance
- support
- understanding
- peacefulness
- security

Summer is also where the roles within the relationship become defined or redefined for those couples that have been together for long periods of time. Routines become established, and there is a strong sense of teamwork, certainty, and stability. With the garden and flower bed flourishing, a simple system of maintenance is all that is required for ongoing success.

Couples who are successful at having extended seasons of summer in their relationships are the ones who have learned to maintain what they have attained. They recognise that the flower bed did not appear without the ecology test, the preparation of the soil, the planting of the seeds, and the nurturing of the relationship. They understand that the enjoyment of summer is also about maintenance, and they operate with an attitude of gratitude and a continued desire to keep growing. They seek new knowledge on growing their relationship and are often the ones attending marriage seminars, reading books, and seeking new activities to keep their relationship growing.

When systems and flow within a relationship are strong, new areas of growth and abundance can be explored. This exploration often leads to the decision to invest in something outside of the relationship, signifying a transition into autumn.

Autumn

While spring is about birthing and creation within the relationship and summer is the reaping of internal rewards, autumn represents a cycle of definition and birthing outside of the relationship, where one plus one equals three. Autumn is about giving love, focus, and attention to something external of the relationship, whether it's the birth of a child, the construction of a new home, or the idea for a new family business. Ideally the focus on the external is made possible by the strong internal foundation set in the spring and summer months. This theme of creation and giving birth to something outside of the relationship was also covered in chapter 3 when we explored the essential tools and core needs of a relationship.

The birthing and focus on the external then naturally leads to the need to nurture and maintain, where roles and responsibilities within the relationship become key. The couple begins to function as a team, and responsibility is increased. It is here during this increased height of responsibilities that the relationship can fall one of two ways. Firstly the couple can establish a functional flow of new responsibilities that allows them to maintain a sense of connection and passion to keep the relationship thriving. While there may be a slight dip into winter during the adjustment period, the functional flow at the new level during autumn will allow the relationship to flourish and return to the spring and summer months. This outcome requires a continued acknowledgement of the importance of the internal relationship before external commitments. Again this was explored further in chapter 3.

However, if the focus on the external becomes the overall focus of the relationship, then the internal connection and passion takes a back seat to the point where these areas begin to break down. This later approach can shift the relationship into a direct state of winter, where the sense of togetherness and connection is lost in a sea of commitments to the external.

Characteristics associated with the autumn season of a relationship can include the following:

- routine
- the definition of roles and responsibilities
- a focus on the external
- boredom
- power struggles
- uncertainty

- blaming
- feelings of being unappreciated
- stress
- feelings of drifting apart
- detachment
- neglect

Just as the seasons of the planet come and go in a natural flow, so do the seasons of a relationship. The difference is how long you spend at each stage. How will you acknowledge your relationship flow and how do you plan for the next cycle to ensure continued happiness and fulfillment?

Relationships are not a lifelong experience of spring and summer. Rather, all relationships will inevitably experience all seasons. How would you know the warmth of summer without the coolness of winter? How would you know the birth of spring without the falling leaves in autumn? As I've mentioned, there can be no light without darkness, no success without failure, no joy without pain. The experience of all seasons is a true gift and unique to each individual couple. The seasons may not be experienced chronologically or for similar lengths of time. Instead the experience of the seasons will depend on the nature of the parties involved in the relationship. Have a think about your own relationship right now. Where do you believe you are at in terms of the seasons of love? If you have been in the midst of winter for some time, perhaps it is time to commit to some relationship growth to rediscover the excitement of spring. Or if you are currently experiencing spring or summer, are you acutely aware of how you intend to maintain these good times for a sustainable period? The fact is that relationships either grow, or they regress. They never stand still. The key question to ask is this: What is the single next thing you need to focus on within your relationship in order to move forward in continued growth?

The Female Dance of Self-Worth

To complement the seasons of love, understanding intimacy cycles allows us to further normalise and embrace the flow of emotion we experience on a regular basis. Rather than tapping into a continual need for high energy and positivity, we can instead acknowledge the flow of our own emotions.

How do these concepts relate? The way I prefer to explain the connection is to picture the seasons of love as a stage in a theater where the backdrop changes depending on the seasonal setting of the act. The lights may dim during winter and rise in the summer. The soundtrack may be thunderous and harsh for the cooler times and then light with birds and waves for the warmer climate. The female and male intimacy cycles are then the performers who dance a routine of their own across the stage of love. While their performances are unique, they are also intimately entwined to create the magic of the show. Understanding the unique element of the way they move is essential in order to learn the dance. When the uniqueness is acknowledged, the performance can then come to life.

Through this metaphor you can see how the seasons of love exist as the backdrop of our relationships, and then the female and male intimacy cycles take place on a daily or more short-term basis. The female and male intimacy cycles continue to repeat regardless of the current season. In this way both performers will experience both highs and lows during winter, spring, summer, and autumn. The intimacy cycles are irrelevant to the current season of love; however, the characteristics of the season may fuel a more rapid high or low within the cycles, depending on the situation of the relationship. It is therefore important to understand both as part of a bigger picture and as part of the circle of life.

The female performer dances a cycle of self-worth where her ability to give and receive love in her relationships is generally a reflection of how she is feeling about herself at the time. Females tend to respond in the moment based on emotional energy. She makes her decisions based on her emotional state of the moment. When she is not feeling great about herself, she is less accepting and appreciative. This low-level dip in the female dance tends to be characterised by feelings of being stressed where common complaints may include the following: "I'm exhausted." "It's just all too much." "I just feel yucky today." These thoughts signify the low dip of the dance, and as a result, her ability to give and receive love diminishes. Unresourceful emotions become easily triggered, and she enters a more vulnerable state where more love is required.

The challenge arises at this point when the male performer has no awareness surrounding this pattern of human behaviour. Many men become incredibly confused and frustrated during the low-level dip of the female dance, causing challenges and relationship breakdowns. One minute she seems so incredibly happy with life, love, and everything in between. Happy wife equals happy life, and he believes he is doing so well. Yet the next minute the dance may be changing, and the low-level dip could roll in and bring feelings of uncertainty and low self-worth. At this point, given that a woman's ability to give and receive love in her relationships is a reflection of how she is feeling about herself at the time, this low-level dip has an immediate impact on the world around her. Suddenly he wonders where it all went so wrong? What happened, and how can he fix it?

But pause the show! This is the first key learning for men when it comes to the female dance of self-worth. It is *not* something that needs to be fixed. The last thing a woman needs when she is on her way down is someone telling her why she shouldn't be down. What she needs instead is someone to be there as her support, to listen while she shares her feelings, and to empathise with what she is going through. It's the hand on the back at the dip of the dance. When she hits her lowest energy, she searches for love and support. When she finds it or chooses to reconnect to it, she then begins to automatically rise up again with increased self-acceptance and the return of her ability to radiate love in her relationships. Men, it's not your job to fix the situation. Rather, your role is to be there as a support to allow her to rediscover love and connection. In everyday life we often see the façade of a corporate suit or social niceties cover up the low-level dip of the female dance, yet in the comfort of her own home when the curtains are down, she is forced to acknowledge her true feelings and emotions of the moment. The key for men is to provide a loving, attentive, and supportive environment through both the high and low levels of the dance.

**A woman's ability to give and receive love
in her relationships is a reflection of how
she is feeling about herself at the time.**

Relationship expert Dr. John Gray cites a study in his work that reveals a woman's self-esteem generally rises and falls in a cycle between twenty-one and thirty-five days. While this time frame averages at a twenty-eight-day cycle, the self-esteem dance is not necessarily in sync with the menstrual cycle. As a suggestion for best understanding the female dance of self-worth, I suggest recording your experiences of emotions over a specific time frame, as you would your menstrual cycle, to better understand your own emotional rhythm and flow. While the masculine "I can take on the world" façade may serve a functional purpose at times, allow it to come down when it needs to and allow your true emotions to come through. Begin to build rapport with your unconscious mind and acknowledge what it is your body is communicating to you. Following this acknowledgement, find fulfilling ways to best serve yourself during the lower-level dips of your dance. Simply trust the flow of what it is you need to be doing to reconnect with your own self-love.

The Male Intimacy Dance

Often we associate cycles of intimacy and mood with females, yet it's important to note that men also experience a dance of intimacy, which addresses the reason men need their space. Attention, ladies. The insights surrounding this need for space will assist you with putting the male intimacy cycle into perspective. Firstly it's essential to understand that men automatically alternate between needing intimacy and needing independence. The performer of the dance goes back and forth across the stage from a state of craving intimacy with the female performer to a rebound state of autonomy. Both feed off each other. Once a man's need for intimacy is fulfilled, he then moves on to seek autonomy and independence. However, when he pulls away, he can only go so far before he comes springing back. The dance is back and forth, getting close, pulling away, and then getting close again with a renewed sense of energy and desire. This is the basis of the male intimacy cycle.

Dr. John Gray uses the term "man cave" to describe the place where men go to reconnect with self and solve their problems through thought during the pull for independence. Man caves can come in a variety of forms ranging from maintaining the backyard to playing in the toolshed to repairing cars, fishing, or other independent hobbies. All man-cave activities have one thing in common—they are done alone. Men need time in their own space to reconnect with their sense of independence, yet often misunderstandings around why men need their space can be the cause of relationship breakdowns. To a certain extent, a man loses himself through connecting with his partner. By feeling her needs, problems, and emotions, he may lose touch with his own sense of self. Pulling away allows him to re-establish his personal boundaries and fulfill his need to feel autonomous. After he fulfills his need for autonomy, he can then reconnect with his hunger for intimacy. Understanding the male intimacy cycle can make all the difference in building a stronger relationship with your loved one.

**To a certain extent, a man loses himself
through connecting with his partner.**

I explored this theory with Hayden and began to get really curious about the ways in which he sought his independence and autonomy as part of his cycle. As we spoke, we reflected on some challenges we had early in our relationship where he used to go into work on a Saturday and spend up to seven hours (yes, seven hours!) cleaning his truck. I used to get frustrated that such a large chunk of our weekend was taken up with him spending time at the truck yard. Yet through our reflections I have now come to understand that this was his time to connect with self and to regain his sense of independence and autonomy. When a man loves a woman, periodically he needs to pull away before he can get closer. By spending time on his own to reaffirm his own sense of independence, Hayden was then able to reconnect with me on a more intimate level, bringing home the best version of himself.

If a man does not have the opportunity to pull away, he never gets a chance to feel his strong desire to be close. My relationship challenges with Hayden were sparked when I used to call him and ask how much longer he would be. I used to then get upset that he would rather spend time alone than together. My interpretation was this: "He loves his work more than me." What I didn't realise at the time was that his ability to reconnect with self and his own sense of independence was directly linked to his ability to love and care for me within our relationship. This may sound familiar as a representation for similar areas within your own love life. Although your situation might be different, the pattern of human behaviour remains constant.

With all of this in mind, there are two ways a woman may interfere with her man's natural intimacy cycle. They are the following: (1) chasing him when he pulls away, which is similar to my example of Hayden and his time at the truck yard, and (2) punishing him for pulling away.

Punishment can often take place through the withdrawal of love and affection and can make men afraid to pull away for fear of not being accepted upon return. This fear can then lead to confusion, resentment, and the lack of fulfillment in both intimacy and independence. This state is not sustainable within a relationship.

However, a man needs to understand that when he pulls away, this has an impact on his partner. Women primarily need safety, protection, comfort, validation, and reassurance. By pulling away, a man can challenge many or all of these needs. With this insight about how women are affected by the male intimacy cycle, a man can recognise the importance of reassurance to reassure her that she is loved, that he cares, and that he will be back. One of the ways Hayden now seeks his man time is through cycling—long bike rides for hours on end. Now that he understands the behaviour patterns and core needs of both men and women, he says things like this: "I'm going for a ride alone, and then this afternoon how about I take you out for a coffee." I get a kiss and an "I love you," while the coffee date works as a reminder that he'll be back when he's ready. Both of us are happy, and the core relationship needs are met.

When we focus on demystifying cycles and patterns of human behaviour to better understand them, then we can truly begin to experience an increased level of understanding and intimacy. Through increased understanding and intimacy, we can then experience a relationship that meets essential core needs, promoting happiness and fulfillment. As a result, the magic of the performance comes alive as the two performers move in an independent yet uniquely entwined way.

Intentional Love

Emotional obsession is the initial stage of romantic love, and research indicates that the average duration of this initial euphoria in a new relationship is two years. After this time we must begin to connect with the next stage of love based on intention and a conscious effort to meet the emotional needs of our significant other. As Dr. M. Scott Peck wrote in his wildly successful 1978 book *The Road Less Traveled*, "The feeling of ecstatic lovingness that characterises the experience of falling in love always passes." He explains how emotional obsession and romantic love is a myth. Real love involves investing ourselves in the needs and desires of another person. "We must be committed beyond the boundaries of the self," he says.

Many relationships fail because couples do not acknowledge the transition from this initial obsession as part of romantic love to the intentional state of love. Instead they blame external circumstances for relationship break-ups. "I'm just not that into him/her anymore" or "we've grown apart" are common phrases you may begin to hear as part of an unsuccessful transition. The three-year milestone in a relationship can often be termed the make-or-break barrier, where the true test of commitment is brought to the forefront. Following the two years of initial euphoria, the relationship the goes through the third year as a transition period from emotional obsession to intentional love. Couples who fail to make the transition may instead become drawn to alternate options, such as attraction to another or separation. It is here where we see relationship break-ups and divorces come in to play. Although it may be some years later that the final break is marked, it is often around this transition period that the initial seed of relationship failure is planted.

Yet a quick jump to the next made bed is not always as appealing as it may first seem. The simple fact is you still must experience the transition period at some point, and chances are the patterns are likely to be repeated in your next relationship. Sixty per cent of those who remarry will experience a second divorce. And if they decide to try again, the divorce rate for third marriages is even higher at 75 per cent.

The link is obvious. The importance of learning how to make the transition from obsessive love to intentional love is essential and well worth the journey.

**Relationships fail when couples do
not acknowledge the transition from
initial obsession to intentional love.**

The second stage of love is truly different from the first. The obsessive feelings you had for each other begin to fade, and you begin to recognise other important pursuits in life besides pursuing each other. Ironically, as part of this journey, you grow into a stronger version of your true self, and it is here that the divine principle of a relationship comes to fruition, where one plus one equals three. Two truly do become stronger as a whole. The intimacy of the obsessive love stage is multiplied and experienced at a whole new level.

Chapter Summary

Along with other key concepts covered in this book, this chapter on the seasons of intimacy provides key tools for assisting the movement from obsessive to intentional love. When you know more, you can do more. When you understand the human behaviour models at play, then you can reflect on your own situation and self-regulate to a state that better serves you. You can have discussions with your lover based on broader patterns of behaviour as opposed to nitpicking personal attacks. Broader, big-picture thinking helps foster agreement.

Feeding our bodies around the kitchen table is a vital metaphor for the seasons of intimacy we experience as part of our relationships. This chapter has covered three main areas significant to the flow of a relationship.

- The seasons of love
- The female dance of self-worth
- The male intimacy cycle

When we are aware of these cycles and can acknowledge the role they play within our relationships, then we can be better equipped to normalise and embrace the flow of emotions we experience on a regular basis. Rather than tapping into a continual need for high energy and positivity, we can instead acknowledge and connect with our own emotional flows.

The restricting cocoon and the struggle required for the butterfly to get through the tiny opening was nature's way of forcing fluid from the body of the butterfly into its wings so that it would be ready for flight once it achieved its freedom from the cocoon. Perhaps the two-year time frame on the initial euphoria within a relationship provides a similar message. Work through challenges as they arise. Don't take the shortcut—the scissor release or the jump to the next available bed. Instead get educated on the levels of thinking and patterns at play. Seek to understand the impacts of these cycles and flows within your own relationship and then use your knowledge to better enhance your situation. Knowledge is power.

Exercises for Reflection

The Seasons of Love: What Season Is Your Relationship in?

Circle the words in the following table that best describe your relationship in its current form. Then total the selected words from each category to discover the highest score that best describes the season where your relationship currently resides.

Winter	Spring	Summer	Autumn
Hibernation	Birthing (internal)	Exploration and growth	Definition and birthing (external)
Loneliness	Excitement	Happiness	Routine
Lack of communication	Optimism	Joy	Definition and roles
Hurtful communication	Gratitude	Satisfaction	Focus on the external
Arguments (often)	Sense of togetherness	Contentment	Consistency
Negativity	Appreciation	Accomplishment	Responsibility
Hurt	Hope	Connection	Boredom
Anger	Love	Growth	Power struggles
Frustration	Trust	Education	Uncertainty
Disappointment	Strong communication	Teamwork	Blaming
Hopelessness	New beginnings	Spirituality	Lack of appreciation
Destruction	Willing to change	Acceptance	Stress
Discouragement	Making plans	Support	Drifting
Emptiness	Alive	Understanding	Burned out
Critical words	Nurturing	Peacefulness	Detached
Coldness	Anticipation	Security	Neglectful
Total:	**Total:**	**Total:**	**Total:**

- Based on your total scores, what season is your relationship currently experiencing?

- What specifically in your life right now tells you this is true?

- Are you satisfied with the season your relationship is currently in? If so, how will you maintain this flow? If not, what season would you prefer to be experiencing right now?

- If you desire a shift, describe the current gap between where you are and where you'd like to be?

- Based on the information in this chapter, what is the one thing you now know that will have the biggest impact in moving you forward towards your desired result?

- If you desire to maintain the experience of the current season you are in, what is the single next thing you need to focus on within your relationship in order to sustain continued growth towards the maintained results you desire?

The Female Dance of Self-Worth: Getting to Know Your Cycle

Get to better know your own female dance of self-worth through the following suggestions:

- Commit to keeping a diary or log to summarise your emotions over a specific time frame, as you would your menstrual cycle, to better understand your own emotional rhythm and flow.

- Focus on building rapport with your unconscious mind and acknowledge what it is your body is communicating to you on a regular basis.

- Brainstorm a shopping list of at least fifteen ways to care for yourself during your lower energy times. To get you started, some suggestions might include taking a hot bath, home baking, reading, journaling, exercising, meditating, and creating art. Complete a list that aligns with your own beliefs and values and go shopping from the list next time you are feeling a dip in the dance, purchasing the activity of choice in that moment to best support you and lead you back to a connection with self-love.

The Male Intimacy Dance: Getting to Know Your Cycle

Get to better know your own male dance of intimacy through the following suggestions:

- Brainstorm a list of ways you seek independence and autonomy.

- Reflect on the list you've created. Are these resourceful ways to meet your needs? If so, how can you further integrate and embrace them in your life?

- If not, brainstorm a list of at least fifteen keys things you might do to seek independence and autonomy in a resourceful way. To get you started, some suggestions might include working on cars or boats, fishing, playing an independent sport, spending time in the garden, hunting, or camping. Complete a list that aligns with your own beliefs and values and detail how you will integrate these activities into your life.

- Knowing what you now know about the impact of the male dance on relationships, have a discussion with your partner about how you might best integrate your need for independence and autonomy into your relationship to ensure a passionate and loving return to intimacy.

Chapter 8

Dinner Conversation: The Power of Communication

The art of conversation is not mediation, negotiation, problem-solving, debate, or public meetings, but simple, truthful conversation where we each have a chance to speak, we each feel heard, and we each listen well.

—Margaret J. Wheatley

Often the source of our problems as couples is not that we don't love and care about each other but rather that we do not know how to communicate well about the things we want and need. A breakdown in communication accumulated over a period of time is one of the major reasons why relationships fail. This chapter addresses communication disconnects and focuses on the power of communication in relationships. Again the humble kitchen table provides the ideal setting for conversations of connection. For many connection over food is a powerful platform on which to foster communication, and the length of a meal provides a convenient time period through which to bond. This soup is delicious. The potatoes are a bit salty. Room for dessert? Among the flow of the dinnertime formalities is an opportunity for increased intimacy, and there are specific ways you can enhance the quality of your dinnertime conversations. For example, you can ensure the ambience is set to encourage a relaxed environment and space for discussion. While there may be background music, it needs to be at a level where you can still hear each other speak. Next choose to embrace open-ended questions. Rather than asking, "Did you have a good day?" which simply requires a yes or no response, extend the opportunity for engagement with a more open approach by saying, "How was your day? Tell me about something that happened today that has made the biggest impact for your moving forward to tomorrow?"

Author Luci Swindoll has a rule that works wonders at her dinner table—and now it works for ours—in that you must always stick to one selected conversation. The idea is to pick a topic and go deep to foster an increased level of intimacy based on conversations that surpass surface-level thinking. Often the most interesting conversations come after the initial question and response, so don't move on so quickly that you miss the gold. Stay and embrace the depth of the topic.

To enhance your relationship right now, this chapter aims to equip you with vital insights for communication success. While the focus is on the context of your most intimate relationship with your significant other, the value gained by engaging with this content will overflow into all areas of your life. Key topics of exploration include the power of language, communication models that reveal the inside secrets on what your lover is *really* thinking, understanding attraction strategies, and the power of anchoring.

The natural flow of a meal should be cherished for the opportunities it provides to both nourish our bodies and our relationships. Too often a good relationship is taken for granted rather than given the nurturing and respect it deserves and desperately needs. Link your daily time at the kitchen table to the nourishment of both your body and your connections. The transformation will be profound.

The Power of Language

"The words we consistently select will shape our destiny." A powerful concept shared by author and speaker Anthony Robbins. It's such a simple drop in the pool of consideration yet such a prevailing notion that has the ability to completely transform your life. That's right. Sit up and take note, as a few simple changes in this space can have an immediately profound impact on the way you experience your world right now. Your words create your emotions, which then create your actions. If you can begin to recognise and take advantage of this link, then you will notice that from your actions flow your results. Cut to the chase. If you want better results, then choose better language. It's a powerful tool for success that's available to anyone willing to take the time to consider the words they use on a daily basis.

Let's dig deeper. Have you ever had one of those days that is full-on from the word go. You get home in the evening, collapse on the couch with a long, outward breath, and claim, "I'm exhaaaauuuusted." In that moment when you voice these words, notice how truly exhausted you begin to feel, for it is following this statement that the emotion is amplified. What would happen if instead in that same moment you chose to replace "I'm exhaaaauuuusted" with "I'm feeling a little low on energy"? Notice the immediate change in reaction from your body and the new way in which you might begin to experience the moment. The words you use can determine just how tired you are choosing to be. In terms of the emotion of anger, what would happen if you were to replace "I'm furious" or "I'm so pissed off right now" with "I'm feeling a little bit bothered." The change in intensity sounds almost comical. Yet the reaction from the body is incredible, where the change in phrase can impact the level of tightness experienced in the chest and intensity in the fists.

The purpose of these examples is not to tell you how to feel but rather to demonstrate the power language can have on your feelings and subsequently your actions. What you do with the insights is then up to you.

The impact of the language in your world around you can be equally as influential. I can recall driving to work one morning after a sunrise workout, fabulous breakfast, and a general high-energy start to my day. As I drove into town, I noticed my energy levels dropping rapidly. I had an exciting day ahead, so I was curious as to why the sudden sleepy feeling had come over me. As I reflected, I noticed the lyrics of the tunes pumping from my radio system. "The Lazy Song" by Bruno Mars sang, "Today I don't feel like doing anything. I just want to lay in my bed. Don't feel like picking up the phone, so leave a message at the tone, because today I'm not doing anything. Nothing at all."

With such a catchy tune, I found myself humming along, and as I noticed the words of the song, I began to question what messages I was feeding my unconscious mind. Could this be connected to the sudden feeling of laziness I was experiencing? It's fascinating when we stop to reflect on the implicit messages that surround us on a daily basis. On that particular morning I made a conscious decision to turn off the radio and instead picked an empowering song from the favourites list on my iPod to accompany me on my drive to work. The key is awareness.

To further demonstrate the power of words, I thought it appropriate to share some of my favourite transitions I've made over the years in consciously choosing more empowering language to define the results I desire. To begin, there are certain words that I no longer use. For example, the word *try* very rarely appears in my vocabulary. Why? Well, think about it. What does trying to pick a chair up look like? The image cannot depict the chair actually leaving the ground, or else that would be an image of *actually* picking up the chair. Instead it tends to be an image of a struggling participant attempting to pick up a chair with no success. As you close your eyes and imagine this scenario, notice the tension associated to the image of trying and the complete lack of results implied by the word. With this in mind, what role does the word *try* currently play in your toolbox of vocabulary?

Stressed is another word I have chosen to remove from my vocabulary as my strategy was not very attractive and wasn't serving me well. The reality is that there are still times when I have a lot of demands coming from multiple areas of my life, and I do tend to feel a certain amount of pressure. The challenge here is the ability to use language to describe the situation yet in a more empowering way. With this in mind, I chose to replace the word *stressed* with *hot demand*, flipping the situation on its head to emphasise a more high-quality challenge where my skills, time, and offerings are now in hot demand. Even as you simply read the words on the page, notice the change in energy associated with each of these words and how the way we choose to language our situations can have such strong impact on the way we then *experience* them.

Another switch in words that is on my favourites list is the transition from *no worries* to *my pleasure*. Isn't it interesting that when we are thanked for completing a task, we often respond, "Oh, no worries." When you stop and reflect on this phrase, it actually presupposes the existence of worries in the first place in order for there then to be none. Is this actually what we intend to say? In my case I realised it wasn't, and instead what I wanted to convey was that it was a pleasure to help. Therefore, I now use *my pleasure* the majority of the time in response to a thank-you.

Language can also be used to presuppose the existence of something. For example, the phrase "I am not financially wealthy" can be changed by adding the word *yet* to read, "I am not financially wealthy yet," presupposing that you soon will be. Say it how you want it, particularly if this is the direction you are choosing for your life. *Yet* is such a simple three-letter word with such a profound impact on the meaning of a statement.

If you find yourself caught in the drama of other people's limiting beliefs, a great way to acknowledge their thoughts without language agreement is through the use of the word *interesting*. My clients and I play with this word a lot. Through this term you are respecting the map of the world for the person who is speaking and then simply responding to what he or she has to say with a term that implies neither agreement nor disagreement. Rather, it is simply *interesting* according to your own map of the world. Again notice the difference in the messaging you are allowing your own unconscious mind to take on, where *interesting* simply implies a reflection as opposed to the need to agree or disagree.

Simply by changing the words you use, you can immediately change how you think, feel, and live. It's such a simple concept with a profound impact, and we all have access to the language we choose and therefore the results we choose to impact. Following the sharing of my own favourite language choices, here are some more language changes to consider in your own journey to embracing more empowering language. Consider the impact of changing the language in the first column to the options in the second:

disappointed	to	underwhelmed
I hate	to	I prefer
pissed off	to	a little bit peeved
stressed	to	in hot demand
exhausted	to	low on energy
lazy	to	storing energy
It's freezing.	to	It's fresh.
frustrated	to	stimulated
afraid	to	slightly concerned

In the same effort you can work to make empowering words even more powerful by turning the intensity up to substitute a word with even more energy. Here are some examples:

great	to	fantastic
good	to	awesome
excited	to	over the moon
like	to	love
satisfied	to	completely content
great day	to	fabulous day
looking good	to	gorgeous
Well done.	to	You're a superstar.
nice work	to	outstanding results

The words you use to describe your experience become your experience. As another example, I often marvel at the way people associate language to specific days of the week. "Monday always drags." "Bring on Wednesday, hump day." "Thank goodness it's Friday." Through these labels we are creating our experiences and the key question to ask yourself is this: "Is this the experience I really want to create?" And if not, then phrase it the way you want it.

The words you use to describe your experience become your experience.

Given these insights on language, let's now have a look at the impact of words in a relationship context. How do you think the results are going to differ for two couples who use the following statements to describe their disagreements: (1) "We always argue," versus (2) "We have a few blips on the radar every now and then." In relationships, the use of generalisations, such as *always* and *never*, are often used in the heat of the moment to communicate extreme frustration and anger. Yet what these types of words do is move the context of the situation out over the entire context of the relationship. For example, the phrase "You never take me on romantic dates" presupposes this has *never* happened or *will* never happen. Is this really what you are intending to say?

Language in terms of relationships also extends outside of the relationship itself, and general conversations should be considered in terms of the ways in which you talk about your lover with others. What language do you use to describe your spouse to your family, friends, and colleagues? What does this presuppose about the way your relationship will continue to develop, given that your language guides your emotions, which then impacts your results? What would happen if you were committed to referring to each other as king and queen? Notice all the connotations that come with these terms and the immediate levels of respect that are associated with these archetypes. Hayden is my king, and I am his queen. These labels shape the way we treat each other.

The ripple effect of this topic is profound, and I challenge you to begin to notice the habitual language you choose from this point forward. The way you communicate with others and with yourself ultimately determines the quality of your life and surrounding relationships. Take these insights and make a commitment within your relationship to hold each other accountable for the language that exists in your everyday worlds in order to foster a relationship playing field conducive to your desired results.

Communication Styles: What's Your Lover Really Thinking?

Shopping for jeans used to be a deal-breaker when it came to our joint shopping ventures, and with every new season it didn't seem to get any better. It was one of those areas where we simply felt we needed to agree to disagree. Let me give you a brief snapshot. One particular shopping trip saw Hayden try on more than twenty-five pairs of jeans, all of which were not ideal according to his strict criteria. Too loose. Too tight. Knees feel restricted. The crotch is out of place. You see, Hayden's jeans must reach the threshold of certain tightness around his waist matched with a certain amount of movement around his thighs and knees. He is also incredibly conscious of the fit around the buttocks area, particularly how the jeans feel as he sits down—and yes, this test comes with some pretty impressive bend and stretch maneuvers. It's all part of his strategy for purchasing his jeans based on his primary need for things to literally *feel* good. The list of needs to meet his threshold seems extensive according to my map of the world. Yet based on my own preaching, I strive to respect his reality. You see, Hayden is incredibly kinesthetic, which means the way things *feel* is of upmost importance when it comes to his buying strategy for clothes. Like Goldilocks and the three bears, things need to fit just right and feel good against his skin.

Welcome to the world of representational systems, also known as communication styles. These titles refer to the way in which we make sense of our world and impact both our style of thinking and the way in which we make decisions. Every day we interact and build relationships with everyone we meet. Have you ever wondered why sometimes you just click when you are communicating with someone? Well, it's most likely that you've established a high level of rapport and are probably matching their primary communication style, reflecting a similar model of the world. When you match and respect someone's primary communication style, you can then begin to increase your potential for empowering communication. If you have respect and understanding of where people are coming from, then you can better tailor your own communication to further guide them and support them to achieve their results. With this in mind, an exploration on primary communication styles is essential in order to better understand what your lover's *really* thinking.

My approach to teaching communication styles is based on the NLP model of representation systems, which looks at the way the human mind processes information through the five primary senses.

1. Visual, what you see and the pictures you create

2. Auditory, what you hear

3. Kinesthetic, what you feel, both internally and externally

4. Gustatory, what you taste

5. Olfactory, what you smell

These simple categories reflect the primary ways you represent, code, store, and give meaning or language to your experiences and the world around you. While you utilise all five of the sensory systems, you also have a preferred representational system that you default to most often. This preferred system impacts the way you perceive your world around you and in turn the way you communicate. By understanding the basic structures of each of the primary senses or representational systems and the characteristics, emotions, and language that come with them, then you can better understand the specific behaviour of individuals.

Understanding the way in which your lover interprets the world around him or her is the key to what your lover's really thinking. It's an incredibly powerful communication model that, when fully understood, brings the intimate gift of increased respect and understanding to further foster intimacy. Before we explore the power within a relationship context further, let's firstly take a closer look at each of the communication styles.

We use our visual, auditory, kinesthetic, and an additional form of logical thinking—our auditory digital system—the most when we are communicating and making sense of our world around us. For the purpose of this chapter I will focus on these four categories as the primary modes of communication.

Auditory digital was not initially introduced as part of the five senses, as this category doesn't directly relate to the senses. Instead it focuses on the human need to make sense of things. It has become a primary mode of communication over the years and is covered further in this chapter. While olfactory (smell) and gustatory (taste) were initially introduced as senses, they are not as relevant when it comes to the study of communication styles. These two modalities will not be explored further and instead serve as general notes of reference. Within each of the four key categories—visual, auditory, kinesthetic, auditory digital—you will have a primary mode of communication, and as you read, you may already recognise the communication style that you tend to rely on most often.

Visual Communication Style

To begin, the visual communication style refers to people who memorise, communicate, and learn by seeing pictures. A visual person is interested in how things look because appearances are important to them. They will often have homes filled with pleasing aesthetics and will be well groomed and presented the majority of the time. Visual people tend to be neat and orderly, and they are often good long-range planners and organisers. They are savvy with colour matching and tend to recognise people by their faces rather than their names. As a generalisation, people in this category tend to speak very fast often because they think in images so have little time to describe the images in their minds. Visual people are strong spellers, as they see the words in their minds. They are also strong readers, once again based on the quick interpretation of words as pictures. In terms of learning, they learn best through pictures and diagrams that detail topics in a big-picture sense. Visual people can often be found doodling on paper during meetings or phone conversations, yet they do pride themselves in the final copy of documents looking neat and tidy. Given the strong pull to communication through imagery, visual people can often have trouble remembering verbal instructions because their minds tend to wander. They remember what was seen rather than heard and can often forget to relay verbal messages to others.

**Visual people memorise, communicate,
and learn by seeing pictures.**

When a highly visual person goes on a dinner date, he or she will be primarily concerned with how the restaurant looks. Does the decor match? How are the meals presented? What are the staff members wearing? They will notice the intricate details related to design and their experience will be altered based on these specifics.

As with all communication categories, the language visual people tend to use is a strong clue in identifying their primary style. You will often hear visual people using or relating to the following types of phrases:

- That looks right to me.
- I get the picture.
- Let's take a look at this.
- What does this look like to you?
- I can see what you are saying.
- My perspective on this is—
- Let's get a mental picture.
- How shall we set the scene?
- This appears to be—
- Let's map it out in a brainstorm.

The level of familiarity you feel towards the listed phrases is a good indicator as to how strongly you relate to the visual category of communication.

Auditory Communication Style

Next is auditory, which refers to the communication style dominantly driven by sound. Auditory people tend to talk to themselves a lot and are easily distracted by noise. They often move their lips and pronounce words as they read, and they like to read aloud. They can repeat things back to you easily and effortlessly and are good at mimicking tone, pitch, and timbre. They also prefer to memorise information by steps, procedures, and sequences as opposed to the preference for imagery for the visual communication style. People who are dominantly auditory tend to enjoy listening to music and talking on the phone. They are talkative, love lengthy discussions, and can often lead conversations through lengthy descriptions on passionate points. They are eloquent speakers and may speak in rhythmic patterns.

Auditory people are influenced by sound.

When a strong auditory person goes on a dinner date, he or she will want a location where the noise is not too chaotic so that he or she can engage in appropriate dinner conversation. The background music will also be important to the auditory person, which again must not be too loud or too quiet. The sounds will add to his or her overall dining experience. You will often hear auditory people using or relating to the following types of phrases:

- That's loud and clear.
- Let's talk this through.

- I hear what you're saying.
- Tell me more.
- I'm all ears.
- As a manner of speaking—
- Let's talk by phone.
- Please can you describe that in detail?
- That sounds good.
- That's clear as a bell.

Kinesthetic Communication Style

While the visual person desires pleasing aesthetics and the auditory person values the sounds in their environment, the kinesthetic person is all about feelings. The learning style for kinesthetic people involves memorising tasks by doing or walking through them to experience each of the parts that make up the whole task. People dominant in this communication style often need to experience the event or task in order to learn it. They will be interested in how things feel to them and will often follow their gut instincts. Kinesthetic people tend to use emphasised gestures and hand movements when they speak and relay their stories. These gestures are a sign of the passion and emotions, the way they *feel* about it, coming through.

As a generalisation, kinesthetic people can be known to speak quite slowly and commonly touch people to get their attention.

They may also stand quite close when in conversation, much closer than a visual or auditory person would. This is because kinesthetic people like to engage with and through the energy of others.

Kinesthetic people are all about feelings.

When it comes to a dinner date, the kinesthetic person will be most concerned with the atmosphere of the restaurant and how it feels. Is the staff friendly, and do they make them feel welcome? Does the combination of music, décor, and lighting set the mood? Are there any experiences that add to the evening like Korean BBQ cook-your-own dinner, teppanyaki food-flipping acts, or a dinner show with entertainment? Kinesthetic people are very much about the experience of the date. You will often hear kinesthetic people using or relating to the following types of phrases with the high use of action-based words:

- I've got a gut feeling about this.
- This feels right.
- This is what it boils down to.
- It's a pain in the neck.
- How do you feel about this?
- Let's get in touch with where this is at.
- Get a grip on things.

- We need concrete evidence.
- I can't get a hold of him.
- Let's dig deeper into this to discover the gold.

Auditory Digital Communication Style

The final of the four communication styles is auditory digital, which is an interesting category, as it does not directly relate to any of our senses. Instead this category is about making sense of things and the application of logic. Some argue that it developed alongside mankind. When man first walked on this planet, he was highly reliant on his senses to find food, to seek shelter, and to escape different forms of danger. To survive each day, he was intimately connected with nature and had little need for facts, figures, or intense logic. Yet gradually as humans developed and accumulated possession, it became increasingly necessary to keep track of developments through logic, planning, and associated systems. Today modern life sees many of us sending and receiving hundreds of emails, texts, and voice messages each day with a strong focus on facts, figures, and logic. In this environment highly auditory digital people spend less time using their senses to be aware of what is happening around them and are instead engaged in the nature of the digital communication.

Auditory digital is about making sense of things and the application of logic.

Auditory digital people will spend a lot of time talking to themselves and will often want to know *how* things work, as they need to make sense of things in their own minds. A lot of conversations go on internally for this communication style, to the point where they may recall having a conversation with someone when it actually just took place in their heads. This communication type prefers to learn and memorise information by steps, procedures, and sequences, and it does not tend to embrace a nature of spontaneity. Logic plays a key role in the decision-making process, as do facts and figures.

In the restaurant this hot date will likely run through the menu choices in his or her head and may even assess the layout and functionality of the menu itself. *How do the meals work, and what should I expect?* You will often hear auditory digital people using or relating to the following types of phrases:

- Where is the logic in this?
- How can we make sense of this?
- The step-by-step process is—
- Let's work out a flow chart process for this topic.
- How specifically does this work?

- Let's break this down into specific steps.
- Is there a procedure for this?
- Let me think about it for a while.
- Let's map out the system and associated checklist.
- How do you know this to be true?

So each of us has a primary communication style that we tend to feel most comfortable communicating with—visual, auditory, kinesthetic, or auditory digital. Simply by reflecting on the previous descriptions, it is likely you have already identified with the category that describes you best. In the same way, it is easy to decipher the communication styles of other people in your life by noticing what words they use when they are communicating. These words as clues are called "predicates" or "process words," referring to the way individuals perceive events in their minds and how they choose to process them through their preferred communication styles. Once you identify a person's process words and associated communication style, you can then make a point to match his or her language when you speak to the individual. You can also match the speed at which the person talks. Visual people tend to speak quickly, auditory and auditory digital at a medium speed, and kinesthetic more slowly. By matching these styles, you can increase rapport and the depth of the relationship.

Have you ever noticed that people's eyes move when they are thinking? In addition to language and process words, eye clues can also be used to determine where an individual is accessing his or her information. This next part of the chapter takes on a bit of a technical slant, but hold on in there, as the information to follow is well worth understanding.

To begin, William James, who published *The Principles of Psychology* in 1890, first suggested that internal representations (communication styles) and eye movements may be related. Yet this observation was not further explored until the 1970s, when, as part of the development of NLP, Richard Bandler, John Grindler, Robert Dilts, and others conducted further experimentation in this area. What they found as part of their neurological research is that eye movement both laterally and vertically is associated with activating different parts of the brain. In neurological literature these eye movements are referred to as lateral eye movements (LEM), and in NLP they are referred to as eye-accessing clues because they give us insights as to how people are accessing information.

What these eye-accessing clues mean is that when we are accessing information for a communication response, we will look towards the communication style we are most dominantly associated with. In this sense, our eye patterns provide valuable clues as to whether we are thinking in pictures, sounds, feelings, or logic and self-talk. For example, if you are making a picture in your mind (V for visual), your eyes will tend to go up to the left or right. When you are hearing sounds in your mind (A for auditory) and interpreting messages through sound, then your eyes will tend to go laterally to the left or right. And finally when you are feeling emotions (K for kinesthetic) or talking to yourself (Ad for auditory digital), then your eyes will tend to look down to the left and right respectively. The following diagram will work to put this into context with Earl's eyes showing the direction your eyes will go to access information based on your preferred communication style.

Communication Styles: Earl's Eyes

Meet Earl.

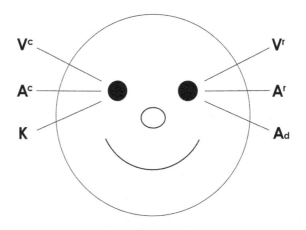

The smaller references to "c" and "r" relate to "constructed" or "remembered" information sources. Constructed means the response requires the construction of new information, while remembered requires accessing a memory that already exists. Earl's eyes are accurate for the majority of the population, yet for some people it has been found that their access to the modalities is reverse organised. This means that the left and right columns simply swap places, where the constructed material is on the right-hand side and the remembered material is on the left as you face Earl or the person you are communicating with. Regardless of the column swap, the key eye signals remain upwards for visual, sideways for auditory, and down towards the ground for kinesthetic and auditory digital. To further embed this learning and to test for yourself, consider the following questions and notice the direction your eyes move. I encourage you to play together with your partner. If your eyes do not seem to move, notice if you have a sense that you are looking in a certain direction, even if only for a fraction of a second.

- **Visual constructed:** Can you imagine what you and your lover will look like in twenty years?
- **Visual remembered:** Do you remember what your loved one wore on your first date?
- **Auditory constructed:** What will your lover's voice sound like in twenty years?
- **Auditory remembered:** Which is louder, the sound of your alarm clock or your doorbell?
- **Kinesthetic:** What does it feel like to hug your loved one? What emotions arise for you?

- **Auditory digital:** When you talk to yourself, what does your voice sound like in your mind's eye?

It is important to note that people's eyes do not always move, particularly for people who have a look-to-talk rule. What happens in this situation is that the person is so focused on holding eye contact, often out of a rule of respect, that while his or her eyes will not appear to move, the individual will instead be defocusing his or her eyes so that the internal eye can look in the appropriate direction to access the information required. Another instance where the eyes may remain steady is when the required answer is easily accessible from the near-term memory. If the answer is something that is well-known to people like names or ages, then they may not need to access the information and can instead verbalise an immediate response.

People have habitual eye movements related to their lead and preferred communication style, which they may automatically default to before they access required information. For example, my primary communication style is visual, so if you were to ask me what it feels like to be married to Hayden, I would most likely see a picture of Hayden and I married first (visual remembered) before I then accessed the kinesthetic emotions associated with being married.

Eye-accessing clues are incredibly powerful communication signs that can allow you to tap in to the maps and levels of thinking of those around you. If you are speaking to people or giving a presentation and you notice that their eyes keep going up to visual, even if you are not using visual language or descriptions, then this is a clue that their primary communication style is likely visual. On the other hand, if their eyes keep turning down to their kinesthetic, then you can presume they are accessing emotional responses to what you are saying or talking to themselves in the auditory digital space if they are reverse organised. With this valuable information, you can consciously choose to direct your conversation to better serve the person's map of the world. This increased respect and rapport for their primary communication system will greatly increase your ability to create powerful communication.

The gold continues as you follow through on applying this knowledge to your love life. In a relationship context these insights can help you understand what your lover is *really* thinking. Picture the couple arguing over holiday plans, where one partner embraces his or her primary kinesthetic communication style, happy to go with the flow of the holiday, while the other lover is primarily auditory digital and would prefer to create a spreadsheet of day-to-day plans to make sense of how he or she will be spending the days.

In the same sense, begin to notice the language that exists in your day-to-day challenges. "You're not *listening* to me!" screams one partner, as the other one reveals similar frustrations by saying, "Because I just can't *see* where you're coming from." The secret has officially been decoded. What you have now is the gift of knowledge, which can immediately recognise the disconnect in this set of statements.

Never again will I simply tell Hayden, "That pair of jeans looks great. Just buy them!" because now I know and respect that it's not about the visual for Hayden. It's the physical feelings. So instead I save my magic words as the change room curtains open and then say, "They look great, handsome, but more importantly, *how do they feel?*" Successful communication achieved.

Attraction Strategies

In addition to the language we use and the communication styles we most frequently relate to, we can also look at everything we physically *do* in life in terms of communication and as a strategy. You have programs for everyday tasks that consist of sequences of thoughts and behaviours triggered by a stimulus. When you can understand how strategies in your life work, then you can begin to review and change your own individual strategies to get less of what you don't want in your world and more of what you do want. The reason that this discussion is so important in the context of relationships and the *Love on the Kitchen Table* model is because the breakdown of attraction strategies is one of the primary reasons relationships fail. During the initial phases of love you are plugged into an attraction strategy that obviously works for you, as it brings the two of you together. Yet as the relationship continues to develop and elements of that strategy may begin to shift and change, your initial attraction strategies may no longer be met in the same way, and in this space the feeling of love and connection can diminish. Yet if you understand the way that strategies work and then apply this knowledge to your relationship, then you can actively ensure you continue to meet each other's attraction strategies as your relationship grows and blossoms.

The breakdown of attraction strategies is one of the primary reasons relationships fail.

In the study of NLP a sequence of thoughts and behaviours that is triggered by a stimulus is known as a strategy. This sequence relates to the specific achievement of an outcome. Take brushing your teeth for example. The way you brush your teeth can be broken down to a step-by-step strategy, one that can be taught and replicated. When you can understand how strategies work, then you can break them down, learn them, and replicate any behaviour you choose based on the specific steps required to achieve that outcome. The best way to think about a strategy is to note the different steps you would need to detail if you were to teach someone else about how you do what you do.

In their work *Plans and the Structure of Behaviour,* George Miller, Eugene, Galanter, and Karl H Pribram discuss how strategies are explored in terms of a four-stage sequence. The TOTE model represents the following four stages: (1) test or trigger, (2) operate, (3) test, and (4) exit.

This order of sequencing was originally based on computer modeling, yet when applied to the more complex structures of human behavior, its simple approach allows us to begin to better understand the strategies for how we do what we do. The study of NLP further developed the TOTE model as a means of describing human processes as a way to successfully model specific behaviours to achieve specific outcomes. It is through this deeper focus on human behaviour that we will explore the concept of strategies.

Taking a closer look at your strategy for how you brush your teeth is an ideal place to begin, as it allows you to first understand how a strategy works so you can then apply it to the context of attraction and relationships. To begin, the first *test* or *trigger* is about establishing the criteria that prompts you to begin the strategy. For example, how do you know it is time to brush your teeth? For some people this may be related to the time of day or to the sequence of their morning routines. For others, it may be a feeling of the tongue on the surface of the teeth, which tells them, "My teeth feel furry. Now is the time to brush." Yet whether it's the time of day or a furry sensation, the trigger is the first step or test that tells you that this is the strategy that will now take place.

The next stage is *operate*, where you are required to access the resources needed to allow the strategy and action to take place. While a toothbrush, toothpaste, and water are all required for brushing your teeth, how specifically you *do* this activity will be unique for each individual. For example, do you wet the toothbrush before you apply the toothpaste, or do you apply it straight to the dry brush? Do you brush top to bottom or left to right? The list of steps goes on, and as you break it down piece by piece, you will discover the uniqueness of your own approach. Each stage of the operation will have its own elements, almost like mini strategies, that make your overall teeth-brushing strategy specific and unique to you.

The third phase of the TOTE model is the second *test*, where you evaluate the effect of the operation or action against the initial test or trigger. The second test is a comparison and will be compared with the first test of the strategy. For example, if your initial test was the feeling of furriness on your teeth, your second test will have you check with your tongue to make sure the intention of removing the furriness has been achieved. If the intended result is achieved, this leads on to the fourth stage, which is the *exit* from the strategy. Yet if for some reason the result of the second test is not achieved, then the TOTE model repeats, and the strategy loops back to more operation (teeth brushing) and further tests until your specific requirements have been met, allowing you to exit the strategy. Exit means mission complete.

I knew when I first set eyes on Hayden that all my boxes were ticked—tall, dark, and handsome. He carried himself with confidence, yet appeared to have a humble, down-to-earth approach to life. This is all what my map of the world told me before we had even spoken. I was a waitress at the time, working to pay my way through university, and when Hayden walked into the restaurant where I was working, I felt instant attraction. So what was it that created such strong emotions at such a rapid rate?

Have you ever noticed a similar instant attraction strategy taking place or felt that instinctive feeling when you are simply drawn to someone? In just the same way you experience brushing your teeth, you also run a strategy for how you experience attraction—and so does your lover. The secret here is that when you can begin to understand each other's attraction strategies, then you can specifically act to meet and deliver on this strategy to ensure continued attraction. What happens so often in relationships is that you get caught up in the day-to-day dramas of life that move you away from that context and initial phase of attraction. While this evolution of the relationship is completely natural, issues arise when you disconnect from the reasons why you fell in love with each other in the first place. This disconnection and inability to satisfy attraction strategies is one of the biggest reasons relationships fail.

Just like brushing your teeth, your strategy for experiencing attraction can be looked at in more detail through the TOTE model. A series of strategic questions can be explored as part of the TOTE model to begin to understand more about how you experience attraction. Take some time to journal your responses to the questions that follow. If the questions feel awkward to begin, just trust whatever comes up for you. Often it can feel strange when you begin to refer to everyday experiences as strategies, and this type of exploration requires a very different level of thinking to that which you may be used to. Remember, exploring your strategy is like teaching someone how you *do* attraction. Simply trust the process. There is no right or wrong. It's simply a discovery process and can take place in any way you choose.

How do you *do* attraction?

Test

- What was it specifically that first attracted you to your partner?
- What was the very first thing you experienced as part of your attraction?
- What was the first thing you noticed about your partner that you loved?

Operate

- What was it he or she said that you loved?
- What was it he or she did that you loved?

Test

- Against what measures did you decide you were experiencing attraction?
- How did you know this to be true?

Exit

- What tells you that attraction has been achieved and allows you to progress to the next stage?
- How specifically do you know you are experiencing attraction?

As you work through these questions, you can begin to see how breaking down the individual parts of how you *do* something allows you to then understand the specific elements that make up the way you experience that event and emotion. When I first met Hayden, one of the things I was most attracted to was the way he took charge and organised the details of our date, including where we would go, what time we would go, and covering the transportation and bill. Working through the attraction questions with your spouse is key because when Hayden heard that this was part of my attraction strategy—to feel taken care of—he then realised how important taking direction was to me in terms of experiencing attraction.

Knowing what you now know, in the same way you explore attraction strategies you can also reflect on the way you experience love as a strategy. What is it specifically that needs to happen in order for you to feel loved? In his work *The Five Love Languages* relationship counsellor Dr. Gary Chapman describes five unique languages or communication types that we use to communicate, express, and interpret love. This exploration is simply another way to look at strategies and can further enhance your knowledge on how you give and experience love. Dr. Gary Chapman describes the following five love languages:

- Words of Affirmation
- Quality Time
- Receiving Gifts
- Acts of Service
- Physical Touch

Words of Affirmation

Words of affirmation refer to the kind words that your partner says to you. Do the words "I love you" warm your heart? Do sexy complements send your head spinning? Notice how what your partner says to you impacts your measurement of feeling loved. Ultimately do words matter to you?

A good way to understand your most preferred love language is to also consider your reaction to the lack of the language. For example, those who experience love through words of affirmation will be left very upset by hurtful words and often hang on to what was said.

Quality Time

This love language is attached to full, undivided attention and involves physically being there for each other. It's about having your partner's full focus with everything else on standby. The quality time element signifies an expression of love that says, "Here I am, right here with you right now, and nothing else matters."

Distractions are a no-no for this love language, and those who most value quality time will be hurt if they feel like they are being put to the side in the list of priorities. Postponed dates or a failure to listen are also particularly hurtful.

Receiving Gifts

For those who speak this love language, the receiving of gifts is the strongest way you experience love. This is not about materialism. Rather, the symbol of love is in the thoughtfulness and effort behind the preparation of the gift where the gesture itself speaks louder than words. The gifts do not need to be big or expensive. Rather, they should be presented as everyday gestures and a constant reminder of love.

A missed birthday or anniversary is a deal-breaker for those who speak this love language.

Acts of Service

The magic words for those who experience love through acts of service are these: "Here, let me do that for you." This love language is about easing the burden of responsibilities and sharing the load through helping each other out. Actions speak much louder than words in this case and should be built into the routine of everyday living.

Laziness, broken commitments, and making more work for those who experience love in this way are all a big turn-off. They cause stress and ultimately translate to a lack of love.

Physical Touch

Hugs and kisses, holding hands, and sitting side by side with bodies touching are all favourite forms of physical touch for this category of lovers. While your mind may jump straight to physical touch in the bedroom, this category of lovers is about more than that and instead includes the small daily gestures as indicators of love. Presence and accessibility are important to this category to allow for increased touch.

Neglect or physical abuse is both destructive and unforgiveable for those who experience love as physical touch.

Although you might identify in some form with all five love languages, there will be one primary approach that triggers your love strategy—the one you prefer the most. Often you give love in the same way you know you experience love—in the same language. However, it is most likely that this is not the love language of your partner, and therefore, your behaviour may not deliver the results you thought it would. Discuss each of the categories described together with your lover and comment on the one that resonates with you most. Once you realise your strategy for experiencing love and find out your partner's strategy, then you can start doing the things and speaking the language that you know will make them feel most loved.

Combine an awareness of your communication style with your attraction strategy and love language, and you have the road map for relationship success. Remember, 95 per cent of the journey is awareness, so once you begin to discover what you don't already know, then the behaviour and results will follow.

The Power of Anchoring

Once the dinner conversations are flowing in a language that respects your lover's map of the world, then it's important to reflect on the setting of the kitchen table in terms of the anchors that are present. Often anchors speak louder than words. In NLP the term *anchor* refers to a stimulus that triggers a specific physiological or emotional state or behaviour. The stimulus may involve a sight, sound, feeling, taste, or smell. The smell of freshly baked scones takes me instantly back to my grandma's kitchen with images of the family waiting patiently as the final items are placed on the table ready for us to eat. Jam and freshly whipped cream immediately come to mind, and I can feel comfort and a sense of security that arises from the smell of fresh scones. In another breath fried onions take me to summer by the pool. Dad, my brother, and Hayden manage the BBQ while my mum, my sister, and I fuss around in the kitchen, wine in hand and preparation underway. The smell of fried onions ignites a sense of excitement for me because it's linked with the warmth of summer and urges to swim and walk around barefoot.

We often associate anchoring with reflex responses. A certain song might trigger a movement. A red light means stop. A ringing phone moves us to answer it. In their work *NLP in 21 Days*, Harry Alder and Beryl Heather claim that without realising it, we actually spend much of our lives slavishly responding to anchors. With this in mind, negative anchoring is one of the major reasons relationships fail. This occurs when responses to daily anchors begin to take on negative connotations and emotions snowball to the point of unhappiness. Yet if you choose to take a proactive approach to managing your state of mind, you can reverse the slavish response and consciously choose to create empowering anchors that trigger your desired responses. In the realm of your relationship, you can choose to create an environment filled with anchors that sets you up for success.

As part of the dinnertime conversation, atmosphere, and experience, a range of visual, auditory, and kinesthetic anchors can be consciously created to enhance connection. In fact, many of the metaphors we've explored in this book are strong anchors that create an environment for *Love on the Kitchen Table*. Candles are visual anchors that ignite intimacy and connection, while saying grace is an auditory anchor that prompts a spiritual connection to gratitude, appreciation, and thanks to a higher source. So now that you are aware of how specific items, sounds, and touches can ignite such immediate responses, I want to explore some ideas for creating empowering anchors in your relationship.

Beginning with visual anchors and the intimacy of the humble kitchen table, I challenge you to become conscious of the visual items that make up your dining room. What images do you have on the wall, and what do they represent? Is the TV in view of the table and if so, for what purpose? Do you take pride in the way the table is set and how it looks? As you begin to assess all the visual elements that make up this space, what emotions are ignited from the visual anchors you have present? More importantly, in order to foster increased intimacy and connection at the table, what additional visual anchors might you add to the room to create a setting for relationship success?

While we are discussing visual anchors, it's important to reflect on the capacity to diminish what were once positive anchors to a reversed state. For example, when you meet someone and fall in love, the visual element of seeing that person on a daily basis increases your intimacy and connection to them, providing the emotions when you see them are positive and install positive anchors—which they usually are in the initial infatuation stages of love. As the relationship develops and the initial infatuation shifts to the space of requiring intentional love, it's important to nurture the positive visual anchors that have been created when you look at your loved one. When couples argue, I strongly advise that you don't look at each other as you battle out your indifferences. What's happening in this space as you stare at your loved one and express your unhappiness is that you begin to anchor the emotions of that moment to the image of your loved one's face. If you continue along this path, eventually all the positive anchors that you've created surrounding your loved one begin to break down to the point where you wonder why you feel so frustrated when he or she simply walks in the room without saying a word. What has happened here is that your partner is now an automatic visual anchor for frustration and unhappiness, as created in your face-to-face arguments. The reality is that disagreements will inevitably take place, and my suggestion is that when they do, you should consciously choose to take a walk and battle it out side by side. This way you are focusing on the same direction, and your visual attention is focused forward on the future as you walk together and discuss your challenges.

In addition to visual anchors, auditory anchors can also create strong responses that instantly trigger emotions. Hayden and I have a playlist that we listened to during our travels through

Europe. Now when we hear a selection of specific songs, we instantly feel the excitement of being on holiday again, bringing up the emotions of adventure and fun we experienced at the time the anchor was created. While the holiday may have been years ago, the power of anchors as emotional responses to specific triggers can last a lifetime.

What are the auditory cues at your kitchen table? Do you have specific music you listen to during mealtimes? Do you have rules or social norms around the flow of dinner conversation? Given what you are now learning about the power of anchoring, are there specific auditory anchors that you are considering creating in your dinning space to further prompt the desired emotions and feelings of love and connection?

Kinesthetic is the emotion or feeling created by certain triggers. Different rooms of the home can be described as anchors for certain physiological or emotional states or behaviours. For example, the bedroom is the space of sex and sleep. The kitchen is for creativity. The lounge symbolizes an area of connection and relaxation. The bathroom is self-care. The office is the space of business and wealth creation. The outdoor area is social and can signify adventure. And the dining room is for socialising and connection. It is wise to create strong anchors around these themes in each area of your home and to be conscious of the anchors you create and the emotions they trigger. Do not mix business and wealth creation with the bedroom, or you will soon see an impact on sex and sleep. You must be conscious of the themes within each room of your home and create anchors that trigger the appropriate emotions. Kinesthetic anchors to support relaxation in the lounge may include soft cushions and a fluffy floor rug. For business and wealth creation in the office space, you may choose a comfortable power chair and footrest with clean, crisp office furniture that makes you feel alert in that space. Anchoring in the bedroom for sex and sleep is explored further in the next chapter.

Outside of the home anchors continue to be everywhere and can also be portable. For example, a favourite pair of shoes you wear may be connected to power and wealth (visual and kinesthetic anchor). A favourite playlist may be your ideal accompaniment for that summer road trip (auditory anchor). A favourite weekend destination may be anchored to feelings of relaxation and peace. Now that you know the power of anchoring, I challenge you to look at all areas of your life and do an inventory of your personal resources. Decide which memory resources will help you bring about the outcome you are looking to achieve. Change your environment, and you change your results.

Chapter Summary

Michael J. Fox so appropriately quotes that "the oldest form of theater is the dinner table. It's usually got five or six people, a new show every night—same players. Good ensemble; the people have worked together a lot." What I love most about this description is the idea of creativity, openness, and honesty that it evokes. There is no set script, just the simple setting of the humble table, and the meal at hand, and the rest is delivered on cue based on the current state of each of the dinner guests. In this setting anything is possible. As I reflect on my own memories formed around the kitchen table, the opportunity for the spoken exchange of thoughts, opinions, and feelings has resulted in everything from laughter and joy through to tears before bedtime—all relevant to the deep state of rapport achieved through this modest setting. It's not about heightened happiness and joy at every moment but instead an honest reflection and sense of support for life in its current state. It's this state of trust that brings life to the power of understanding language, communication styles to build increased rapport, attraction strategies, and anchored reactions. Weaved with trust and understanding, dinner conversation is an opportunity to embrace the silence when needed and to open up to magical moments of connection as the impromptu theater calls for it.

Exercises for Reflection

The following exercise is designed to increase your awareness of your own preferred communication style and that of your partner. When applied to your daily communication, the insights gained from this exercise can have a profound impact on your ability to increase your understanding and respect for your loved one's map.

Identifying Your Communication Style

For each of the five questions, place a number next to the phrase to indicate your preference and initial response, where four equals "resonates the most" through to one, which equals "resonates the least." Each question should have four responses to the statements based on the categories below:

4 = resonates the most

3 = next best description

2 = next best

1 = resonates the least

Work through the questions one person at a time and then compare your results at the end.

1. **I make important decisions based on the following:**
   - gut feelings and going with the flow.   _____
   - whichever way sounds best to me.   _____
   - whatever looks best to me.   _____
   - precise review and study of the situation.   _____

2. **During an argument I am most likely to be influenced by the following:**
   - the other person's tone of voice.   _____

- if I can see the other person's point of view. _____

- the logic of the other person's argument. _____

- if I am in touch with the person's feelings. _____

3. **My review of a restaurant is most likely to be influenced by the following:**
   - the décor and presentation of the meals. _____
   - the atmosphere and general feel of the place. _____
   - the price, menu details, and venue logistics. _____
   - the music they play and ambiance. _____

4. **It is easiest for me to do the following:**
   - find the volume and tuning on a stereo. _____
   - research and analyse data. _____
   - select the most comfortable furniture. _____
   - select rich, attractive colour combinations. _____

5. **Which of the following statements resonate with you most?**
   - I'm attuned to the sounds of my surroundings. _____
   - I'm good at making sense of facts and data. _____
   - I'm sensitive to the feel of clothing on my body. _____
   - I have a strong response to colours and design. _____

Take the responses from each of the five questions and list them in direct order in the following table. For example, if your response to question one was four, two, one, and three in that order, then list the numbers under the question-one heading.

Consider this example:

1. **I make important decisions based on the following:**

   - gut feelings and going with the flow.   **4**
   - whichever way sounds best to me.   **2**
   - whatever looks best to me.   **1**
   - precise review and study of the situation.   **3**

Question 1	Question 2	Question 3	Question 4	Question 5
4 (K)	(A)	(V)	(A)	(A)
2 (A)	(V)	(K)	(Ad)	(Ad)
1 (V)	(Ad)	(Ad)	(K)	(K)
3 (Ad)	(K)	(A)	(V)	(V)

Next use the following table to add up the numbers associated with each of the communication styles. Once again an example for question one has been detailed below.

	Visual (V)	Auditory (A)	Kinesthetic (K)	Auditory Digital (Ad)
Question 1	1	2	4	3
Question 2				
Question 3				

Question 4				
Question 5				
TOTAL				

The total for each of the categories will give you your relative preference for each of the four communication styles. Compare your results with your partner and explore the following questions together:

1. What are your thoughts on the results you received? Are they what you expected?

2. What specific things in your life right now reinforce these results as true?

3. How do your results differ between the two of you, and what impact do you recognise this has on communication within your relationship?

4. What is the biggest insight you are taking from this exercise or from the contents of this chapter?

5. What specific changes might you now choose to make within the context of communication in your

relationships, given you are now aware of each other's primary communication style?

Exploring Your Strategies for Attraction

If you don't stop and take the time to understand your strategies for how you live life, then you are never consciously aware of how these strategies can be best fulfilled. To explore your strategies for love and attraction, spend some time on your own brainstorming your thoughts on the following four questions and get your partner to do the same.

1. What was it specifically that attracted you to your partner?
2. What was the first thing you noticed about your partner that you loved?
3. What was it he or she said that you loved?
4. What was it he or she did that you loved?

After you complete these questions, share your answers with each other to learn what specifically it was about you that he or she was first attracted to. Now here is the magic! By finding out what your partner's attraction strategy is, you can then act to meet and deliver on this strategy to ensure continued attraction and vice versa.

Chapter 9

Temptation for Dessert: Keeping Sexual Desire Alive

Passion—all you need is your heart
and a little creativity.

The table is built and set with the ideal foundations for relationship success, and the energy of the room is in harmony with an increased understanding and sense of respect for one another. Next it seems entirely appropriate that this chapter completes the *Love on the Kitchen Table* model as the icing on the cake or the cherry on top as the finishing touch for exploring key elements of a successful relationship. In cultures around the world dessert or pudding is a course that typically comes at the end of a meal, usually consisting of sweet food. For some it's a nightly ritual. For others it's a rare treat. To bring the fiery energy to the setting of *Love on the Kitchen Table*, "Temptation for Dessert" explores the spark of sexual intimacy and the passion required to keep sexual desire alive.

There is a common belief in society that a cycle of declination exists when it comes to sex in relationships. A relationship is said to typically start out hot and heavy with a "can't keep my hands off you" sexual urge. This initial phase involves taking every opportunity to grab a quickie and to embrace regular, much longer intimate sessions of lovemaking that explore the depths of possibilities. Yet as the cycle of declination suggests, fifteen years later—following a house, a dog, and a mortgage—most couples struggle to remember the last time their sex life hit an adventurous peak. The cycle presupposes this is what we should expect to experience as part of our relationship based on a belief that passion dwindles. But what if you choose to take a different approach? What if you choose to commit to keeping the passion alive, supporting ultimate fulfillment in your relationship?

This chapter flips the cycle of declination on its head and takes the passion element to a whole new level. Passion is not something to dwindle away after only a few short years of commitment. Instead it's a vital element of a successful relationship, and one that must have energy directed at it in order to keep it alive. As mentioned in chapter 6, the initial chemical reaction and emotional obsession of new love fades after about two years. At this point a conscious effort is required to connect with the next stage of love and romance based on intention and an effort to meet the emotional needs of your significant other. In order to meet these needs, you must know what they are, which we explored in chapter 3, "The Relationship Plate of Core Needs". The purpose of this chapter is to further build on the passion element that we have already touched on, to gift you with knowledge for exploration in the bedroom. When you know more, you can do more. There is a unique gift in an intimate connection fuelled by passion, one that transcends physical barriers, delivering fulfillment to the asymmetry of both masculine and feminine energies. A unique gift worth exploring.

Why Opposites Really Do Attract

Can I have permission to take this to the next level? Rather than focusing on the "he likes the snow and she prefers the beach" basics, I desire to turn up the intensity and look at what it *really* means to have opposites attract. I desire to plant the seed for further reflection on creating passion in your relationship through polarity because passion is a fundamental building block for a successful relationship and must be maintained in order to keep the connection alive. The concept of opposites attracting is key in understanding the power of passion. The two parties within a relationship are seated at each end of the kitchen table, each in their own energy of masculine and feminine. The magnetic force between the two opposing energies vibrates across the tabletop, through the legs of the structure, and out to create a spherical glow of energy surrounding the event. The love, passion, and desire give life to the setting outside of any explainable force. Through this opposing yet mutually beneficial power, the ultimate gift of creation is possible.

Sexual attraction is based on sexual polarity, which is the force of passion that arcs between the masculine and feminine poles. In David Deida's book *The Way of the Superior Man*, he details how all natural forces flow between two poles. The North and South poles of the earth create a force of magnetism. The positive and negative poles of your electrical outlet or car battery create an electrical flow. In the same way masculine and feminine poles between people create the flow of sexual energy. This is sexual polarity. It is here where opposites really do attract, and the attractive difference between the feminine and masculine energies becomes the key for ongoing passion.

Sexual attraction thrives on sexual polarity.

Masculine and feminine energy have been key themes throughout this book and were covered in more detail in both chapter 4 and chapter 5. As a brief review, the yin (feminine) energy refers to the state of being as a receptive power of unity, connection, and relationship. The opposing yet equal force of the yang (masculine) energy is the state of doing. It is external, active, and direction-focused. One energy is not better or supposed to dominate the other. Rather, they work in flow, where the raw energy or pressure meets the passive and receptive force that brings about creation.

The rise of feminism is at the core of this discussion with three distinct classifications, which we touched on in chapter 1. As a quick recap, the three categories include the following:

1. First wave, nineteenth-century suffragettes
2. Second wave, 1960s feminists
3. Third-wave feminists who today prefer the term *women's movement*

Without delving into the history too deeply, the overarching theme to note for the purpose of understanding this chapter is the basic movement towards female rights and the magnifying of the inner masculine.

As a society, we've witnessed the trend toward sexual similarity, where we are choosing to seek a more balanced approach and become more like one another. In their book *The Flipside of Feminism*, Suzanne Venker and Phyllis Schlafly make the point that society now positions men and woman as the same with equal rights, equal lifestyles, and equal opportunities. While this in itself is not necessarily a bad point, in the process we have created a sexually neutral zone, where friendship and love may thrive yet passionate sexual attraction fades. The reason the sexual attraction fades is because it relies on the passion between the feminine and masculine poles. It relies on the acknowledgement and celebration of gender roles and the essence of difference as the opposing force that fuels attraction. It is here in the depths of passion and intimacy where opposites really do attract. Yet instead, as a society, we no longer acknowledge or celebrate the differences between men and woman, and in many cases doing so is frowned upon. The balance has shifted to a fight for power and rights. When power for our rights is fought for from both sides through a combative masculine approach, we have the clash of strength and power through conflict. With this clash, it's not surprising the divorce rates have risen significantly over recent decades. The constant push for sameness and superiority has overridden the magical and unique characteristics of both male and female. In the push for equality we've disregarded what fuses us together in the first place.

The topic of masculine and feminine energy and the impact on our society and relationships is incredibly detailed. My intent throughout this book has been to simply raise the discussion into your conscious awareness for further consideration in terms of assessing the sexual polarity and passion within your own relationship. When you seek to create an equal balance of energy in your everyday life, you create a sexually neutral zone that destroys sexual desire. While a balance in flow is functional most of the time, you must embrace a different approach when it comes to adventures in the bedroom to take on roles and harness energy that best ignites the passion between the feminine and masculine poles. This is true in homosexual as well as heterosexual relationships. The sexual polarities are independent of gender. When you truly grasp the power surrounding opposing energies, then you can begin to make changes and step into energy roles within your relationships to further fuel passion and desire.

Sexual Archetypes

Sexual archetypes provide a simple platform for better understanding how you might choose to embrace a more feminine or masculine role in the bedroom to increase polarity and passion. It has been said that sex is 80 per cent in the mind and 20 per cent physical. What this means is that it's really the imagination that is driving the chemical reaction and attraction through sex. Therefore, the more you can increase the access to imagination that supports sexual activity, the more you can experience sexual passion on a whole new level.

So what are archetypes, and how do they work? Twentieth-century psychiatrist Carl Jung further developed Plato's "elemental forms" concept to first term the series of universal symbols of behaviour as archetypes. Carl Jung's work advanced original thinking to a clearer focus on psychological archetypes and identified key archetype sets within the framework. An archetype is now a universally understood symbol, a term, or a system of patterns of behaviour upon which others are copied. Archetypes are the spiritual lenses though which we view ourselves and our world around us. A specific archetype refers to a generic version of a personality. For example, a *warrior* is considered an archetype of strength, protection, and direction. A man wanting to achieve more masculine energy in reaching his vision and purpose in life may activate his warrior archetype and take on these characteristics. Accessing the archetype is simple. Awareness is 95 per cent of the journey and involves knowing what archetype you need to fire up to get the results you are looking for. Next you can tap into popular culture examples of the archetype you would like to embrace. If you are looking to connect with your inner warrior, you may watch popular films like *Gladiator* or *Braveheart* to model the particular characteristics that make up the warrior's pattern of behaviour. Archetypes can be accessed through role play, language, activities, and the development of new skills through education.

**Archetypes are the spiritual lenses though which
we view ourselves and our world around us.**

While you may relate to a range of archetypes in various ways, you do not have an endless list of archetype sets within you. Instead, as Caroline Myss explains in her book *Archetypes*, "You have a cluster of archetypes that are particular to you, forming your Inner-net of influences that express themselves singly and at times blend their energy." Caroline Myss details ten modern-day archetypes in her work, including the following:

1. the advocate
2. creative
3. athlete
4. rebel
5. caregiver
6. visionary
7. king or queen executive
8. spiritualist
9. fashionista
10. intellect

As you scan through this list, you may already begin to resonate with the archetype sets that describe you best. We don't begin our lives knowing who we are or why we operate the way we do. Instead we have to search deeply for that type of knowledge. Caroline Myss explains how discovering your archetypes is like being introduced to yourself at the soul level, where you then harness a means to express the true reason you were born. Outside of the contents of this chapter, if you are interested in learning more about the power of archetypes, I would highly recommend you review Caroline's work further.

While extensive lists of archetypes exist in modern society, for the purpose of this chapter and in the context of creating sexual passion, I am going to focus on just six main archetypes or characters that are present in a healthy, creative, and passionate sex life. Increased understanding on the characteristics of these archetypes can assist in creating sexual polarity in the bedroom, bringing about increased spark and passion. The exploration of these archetypes is not a reflection of who you necessarily are on a daily basis but instead is a set of characteristics that you can choose to embrace in an intimate setting to ignite sexual passion. Keep in mind that you have a cluster of archetypes you can draw on at specific moments, and the exploration of the following archetypes simply details ideas for types of characteristics you may choose to embrace.

The three strong female archetypes that we will be exploring in relation to sexual passion include the following:

1. Courtesan
2. Seductress
3. Dominatrix

The three strong male archetypes that we will be exploring in relation to sexual passion include the following:

1. Toy Boy
2. Seducer (or Sensualist)

3. Alpha

As we look at each of these archetypes in more detail, notice which of the characteristics you and your loved one currently resemble the most. Naturally as with all archetypes, they have both positive and negative connotations, and their places in society can sometimes be shrouded in the shadows of the negative. However, my challenge to you is to shift your thinking to view the positive attributes of each of the characters, focusing on how the archetypes can deliver an increased sense of passion and romance in your love life. It's not about taking on the complete identity of these characters but instead simply accessing key characteristics to bring out your own inner sex god or goddess.

Courtesan

One of the strongest female archetypes, as part of the sex goddess energy, is the courtesan. Also known as the mistress, modern-day language terms this archetype as the flirt or whore. Yet the references are not meant in a demeaning sense and instead refer to the submissive yet powerful energy of this archetype. The courtesan is a symbol of our spiritual history in which a woman rose to her fullest expression and power by using her erotic nature to do so. She was not free from the patriarchal culture. Rather, she thrived within it as one of the most highly educated and influential women of her time. As an archetype in the bedroom, the courtesan aims to please with polite bedside manners and a yes approach to doing what she's told. At the same time the courtesan is incredibly powerful and can hold her own through her grounding energy. As a beautiful, receptive energy, the vulnerability and openness of this archetype is incredibly attractive.

Seductress

The next prominent female archetype is the seductress. This character encompasses more direct power energy with a focus on seducing the male energy through appealing to the senses and alluring acts of attraction. The word *seduction* stems from the Latin language and literally means "to lead astray." Seen positively, seduction is simply a process of deliberately enticing another person to engage in sexual behaviour. The charm of her voice, the grace of her manners, and the perfume of her lips are some of the ways she lets him know she's interested. Seduction is a synonym for the act of charming someone with the goal of intimacy. The seductress's image, presence, imagination, and performance elicit the immediate attention and admiration of many men.

Dominatrix

Thirdly the dominatrix is another powerful female archetype. Taking the lead role in bondage and acts of sexual discipline, this female archetype is characterised by external strength and power. Particular attire and props are associated with this archetype, including thigh-high boots or stiletto heels with fishnet stockings, seamed hosiery, and leather suspender belts. As a match, the props she may brandish will strongly signify her role as dominatrix, such as bearing a flogger whip or riding crop in conventional representation. One of the ubiquitous garments associated with the dominatrix archetype is the black leather female catsuit. It accentuates and exaggerates the sexualised female form, yet at the same time it provides an obstructing physical penetrative access and plays on the idea of "you can look but you can't touch." This core theme is common to the dominatrix archetype, and while the catsuit is an extreme expression of this set of characteristics, more subtle expressions exist along a continuum. With all the archetypes, the expression or extent to which you tap into them varies depending on your own personality type.

The ability to tap into a range of archetypes adds a beautiful variety to sexual intimacy, along with a sense of exploration and playfulness. Having now read about the three female archetypes, you are likely already beginning to understand the power of the characteristics and the archetype you most commonly associate with. Yet do you embrace variety, and what is the preference of your lover? Sizzle between the sheets can be greatly enhanced when you step out of your comfort zone and experiment with new roles.

Toy Boy

In terms of the main archetypes for men, the toy boy, seducer, and alpha all bring out his sex drive. The toy boy is the most playful of the three. He brings a light-hearted approach to the bedroom and an eager sense of exploration. He takes sex to new, exciting locations with a drive towards fun and adventure. This archetype is eager to please and while modern-day representations of this archetype show physically younger men, the energy of this young essence can be adopted at any age to bring this sense of enlightened youth into the bedroom. The toy boy's light-hearted approach to sex often leads to increased variety and adventure, taking the relationship to new levels. The typical toy-boy archetype is associated with images of strong, athletic men.

Seducer

The next prominent male archetype is the seducer. Like the female seductress, the seducer entices females through sensory acts with the underlying goal of appeasing his sexual desires. Both men and woman can be the seducer or the seduced. The seducer has the ability to focus entirely on his target, giving her his full, undivided attention. Human beings have a multitude of senses, including sight, hearing, taste, smell, and touch. The pleasure-orientated seducer is usually a master at flirtation and understands woman and their feelings. This assists him in drawing his target into his world of sensual experience. A good seducer enables his partner to totally surrender to reach the highest levels of sensation in a safe and supported environment.

Within the seducer archetype, there are different personality blends and traits you can select to best suit your own personality. As an example, a further extension on the seducer archetype is the sensualist. The sensualist does not necessarily need to conquer his target through sex, and instead this individual is more focused on romance. The sensualist notices the finer details of creating an environment for sex, such as the dim of the lighting, colours of the furnishings, and texture of the sheets. The sensualist sees the bath as more than just a way to get clean and is happy to explore the depths of the body and foreplay without the exploration necessarily needing to lead to sex. The key focus is excessive devotion to sensual pleasure, and often the sensualist is more focused on his partner reaching sexual peaks than he is on himself.

Alpha Male

The third primary male archetype in the discussion of sex is the alpha male. Driven by direction and control, he knows exactly what he wants and when he wants it. Dominance and power is key for this archetype, and often force is used to take her how he chooses. The alpha male was born to lead and has conquered his way to the top. He's tough, decisive, and goal-orientated with a sometimes overbearing and inflexible nature. In popular culture James Bond is the ideal example of the modern-day alpha male. With his strong, confidant posture and approach to the mission at hand, his air of authority is incredibly attractive to interested females. Unlike the seducer, the alpha male is not always a great flirt or communicator when it comes to his relationships. Yet his confidence and sense of control makes him incredibly attractive.

The selections of archetypes I have shared open up increased opportunities for connecting with your inner sex god or goddess and creating variety in the bedroom. I encourage you to explore these categories to create a hybrid of options for your bedroom toolkit. You can then begin to understand how they might best serve you on a daily basis. Would you do it on the front doormat by a pile of smelly shoes? My initial reaction was this: "No, that's where people walk, and it's so dirty." As I spoke with my friend about my initial reaction to Hayden's attempt at a quickie on the front doormat, she was shocked at my thoughts.

"Really?" she questioned. "Was that your first thought? How did that even cross your mind? If it were me, I'd be thinking, *He wants me so bad, and we have barely made it through the front door. Take me right here. Right now. That's so hot!*"

This is the perfect example of sexual archetypes at play. Hayden was in the alpha space and knew what he wanted right there and then. However, on that particular day I was looking for more of the seducer or sensualist, craving silk sheets, comfy surroundings, and a bit more of a lead-in. Needless to say the sexual sparks did not fly that afternoon. We had no idea then about the power of archetypes. Had I known, I would have been able to quickly identify where he was coming from and then draw on my own hybrid of sex goddess thinking (most likely the courtesan) to create the sexual polarity required in the moment.

Most couples never break their thinking down to this level or have the discussion around what they prefer in the bedroom and what turns each person on the most. As a result they experience rejection, confusion, and a lack of ability to understand and please the other person at a peak sexual level. Instead they settle for bread-and-butter sex, never exploring the realms of possibilities often because of a lack of education and communication within the relationship.

Archetypes carry tremendous amounts of energy. When an archetype surfaces and we get in touch with the power of the particular personality qualities, we can then begin to understand much more about our own psyches. By allowing ourselves to open up to the meaning of the particular archetypes, we can begin to collate a hybrid personality that best serves our relationships when it comes to creating intimacy, passion, and sexual polarity in the bedroom.

The Power of the Body

While archetypes refer to a generic version of a personality and taking on the mindset or behaviour of a particular character, this next section takes a more external approach and explores the physical make-up and power of the body. Simple insights in to the physical characteristics that attract both men and women to the opposite sex can provide you with a deeper understanding of sexual desire and its innate purpose. This increased understanding of the way in which your body attracts your significant other can then help to further develop your own understanding of physical elements that play a role in attraction.

As we explored in chapter 8, understanding your own unique attraction strategy is important. When you can phrase what it is that makes you attracted to someone, you can then identify the patterns of human behaviour that lead you to fall in or out of love. Unfulfilled attraction strategies are one of the major causes of relationship breakdowns. They are the reason people search for love outside of their relationship, following comments like "I'm just not happy anymore" or "I just can't remember what I ever saw in him/her."

My intention is that this section on the power of the body will gift you some fascinating insights that will assist you in better understanding both you and your partner's attraction strategy. You can then get curious and explore through discussion with your loved one exactly what it is about your body he or she is attracted to. Is he or she a bum, breast/chest, or legs lover? What outfits do you wear that accentuate his or her favourite body part? What is your loved one's strategy for experiencing attraction? The purpose is not that he or she shapes who you are or what you look like but instead that you become equipped with the knowledge about what drives the way he or she experiences attraction. If you want to be more attractive to your loved one, you can then choose to incorporate these new insights into your own unique style.

So what can the body tell us about the way we experience attraction? Relationship and body language experts Allan and Barbara Pease provide an in-depth review of the body and its ability to communicate in their book *The Definitive Book of Body Language.* The common themes illustrated through their work highlight courtship displays and attraction signals that relate back to the core purpose of humans as monogamous creatures designed to form pair bonds to rear young. To support this relationship, we've evolved with different brain systems, which include the sex drive, romantic love, and attachment system. When you begin to understand the brain, it becomes explainable. You can then begin to comprehend and appreciate the way in which the brain's systems for love and intimacy can be triggered by all kinds of things, including specific parts of the body.

What is all the hype about bums, breasts, and legs for men? Let's begin with bums—the buttocks. The female human buttocks differs from other primates in that other primate females display enlarged, protruding buttocks only when they are ready for mating. Human females, on the other hand, have their protruding buttocks on permanent display, communicating an open, sexually available state always. Often women want to lose weight from this part of their body or are conscious about the peach-shaped curves that form the buttocks area. However, keep in mind that it is this shapely, curvy feature that men find so attractive. In all primate species the male approaches the female from the rear and uses her swollen red buttocks as a signal that she is ready for mating. Humans are the only exception to this rule, where we also mate face-to-face. The primitive nature of this attraction insight is the key to men's attraction to women's bums. On an unconscious, primate level, the protruding female buttocks gives the impression that she is available and ready for him always.

I used to wonder what Hayden's attraction with me in the kitchen was. Often when I was preparing a meal or pottering at the kitchen bench, he would approach me from behind and begin to kiss my neck in an incredibly turned-on state. Was it his anticipation of the meal I was preparing? Far from it. I now realise the key driver was the view of my backside as I focused on the task at hand. His interpretation—she is ready and waiting, available for me always. This open state supports regular human sexual activity, designed to encourage long-term pair bonding for the successful rearing of children. The buttocks area also stores fat for breastfeeding and acts as backup food storage in lean times, similar to a camel's hump. The overarching theme is this: Embrace the buttocks. It's a very useful body part.

Female breasts are very closely linked to this fascination with the buttocks area, and Allan and Barbara Pease's work on body language states that the enlarged female breasts have evolved overtime as a mimic of the female rear. Tests conducted with snapshots of bum cracks and breast cleavage convincingly shows that most men are unable to tell the difference between one crack and the other. When a woman walks towards a man, he is unable to see the buttocks area because she is facing him. However, he is instead faced with its replica in the form of breasts. These sister features allow a male to recognise a female from either the front or back, increasing the accuracy and intensity of the attraction strategy. It is the cleavage that stimulates the attraction triggers the most, highlighting the driver behind low-cut necklines and push-up bras. The art of flirting also often revolves around the accentuation of the cleavage line. A woman who is attracted to a man is likely to lean forward and bring her arms closer to her body, which presses her breasts together and highlights her cleavage.

Thirdly the appeal of long legs is a key feature as part of the male attraction strategy. Once again long legs act as a nonverbal cue that communicates an open and ready state of sexual maturity. When a girl reaches maturity, her legs undergo rapid lengthening as hormones pour through her body and change her into a woman. Her extra-long legs become an influential nonverbal signal that tells a male she is sexually maturing and is now capable of childbearing. The combination of these body language insights can increase our understanding of stable fashion items. For example, the high heel has historically given the illusion of having fertile-looking legs. The structure of this shoe also enhances a woman's sexual shape by lengthening her legs, arching her back, and forcing her buttocks to protrude. Skinny jeans can have a similar impact, guiding a particular focus on the buttocks area with the tight-fitting style and shape. The male interpretations of these signs are "she is ready and waiting for me" and "I am wanted, needed, and appreciated"—the core needs of the masculine.

Human behaviour is much simpler than we realise. Based on primate themes of attraction for reproduction, our bodies are designed to foster pair bonding for the successful rearing of our young. The same key body areas in men communicate a similar attraction strategy for females; however, the different meanings align with the core needs of the feminine—love and protection. For instance, a small, compact bum is a favourite feature on men for women. On an unconscious level the tight, muscular rear communicates an ability to make the forward thrusting motion necessary for the transfer of sperm during sex. This athletic feature promises a better chance of doing an effective job as opposed to a fat or flabby make-up that can demonstrate a difficulty in maintaining the thrusting movement. The overweight male frame can also be uncomfortable for the female, as the tendency to throw the entire body into the thrust can squash the female physique, working against the core need of the feminine—protection.

The upper chest area of a man's body is wide and tapers to narrow at the hips. Men evolved these features to allow them to haul heavy items over long distances and to carry home the prizes of their labour. This body feature is very closely connected to a man's ability to hunt and provide and is the reason why women find broad shoulders and muscular chest and arm areas so attractive. Large chests also house large lungs, demonstrating the ability to breathe more efficiently when one is running and chasing prey across long distances. Traditionally men with large chests have commanded more respect and power, and on an unconscious level this body symbol continues to attract females based on these premises.

Men's legs communicate a similar attraction point as symbols of masculine power and endurance. The powerful, angular legs of the human male are the longest of all primates, allowing him to run effortlessly over long distances to chase and hunt. In their work *The Definitive Book of Body Language* Allan and Barbara Pease state that even in the twenty-first century, surveys show women still want a man who looks as if he can wrestle animals, carry heavy things, and fight off invaders.

Body language is a powerful part of courtship because it reveals how available, ready, and enthusiastic we are. Love must be acknowledged as a verb, and if you want to experience it more often, then you must *do* it more often. You need to get curious and begin to play with what it means to you and your loved one to experience physical attraction. What is it about the way you dress and act that really gets your partner going? I've acknowledged some fundamental body parts and referenced their place in evolution as key support tools for pair bonding and the rearing of our young, yet there is more to consider. For instance, how do you dress and present these body parts, and what do these choices say about your masculine and feminine energy?

Take a moment now to reflect in your mind's eye on the current contents of your wardrobe. What are the key colours that are featured there? As a female, do you embrace more feminine, flowing materials, colours, patterns, and dresses, or does your wardrobe represent more sharp-edged pants, suits, and collars? As a male, do you dress like a man or a boy? Are your shirts pressed and mature or covered in childlike art and imagery? What do your clothes say about you?

My intention is not to tell you how to dress and present yourself but rather to trigger the conversation starter with you and your partner. Ask your partner what it is they prefer. Short or long hair? Pants or dresses? Black and grey or colours? Plain designs or patterns? Have a conversation about what these items and body parts symbolise to each other.

Love must be acknowledged as a verb.
If you want to experience it more
often, you must *do* it more often.

While the external features of the body play a key role in creating sexual desire, there is a lot happening internally as well. Extensive research details the importance of chemicals released in the body during intercourse. Firstly testosterone, which exists in both men and woman, is the energy that fuels your sex drive and aggression. This energy is incredibly important during the lead-up to sex to create strong attraction. Next incredibly high levels of adrenaline are released, increasing your heart rate, dilating the arteries, and intensifying blood flow to your muscles. This release of adrenaline ensures you have the energy and strength to make love.

In addition, other chemicals released during sex, orgasm, and post-orgasm have incredibly positive effects on the body. Phenylethylamine, often referred to as the "molecule of love," triggers the release of dopamine in the pleasure centres of the brain during sex and peaking at orgasm. This release triggers the intense feelings of bliss, attraction, and excitement experienced during sex, causing the emotional feeling of being on cloud nine without a care in the world. At the height of orgasm oxytocin is released, often referred to as the "cuddling hormone." As the name suggests, oxytocin causes the warm, cuddly feeling of relaxation. Dr. Norman Doidge in his work *The Brain that Changes Itself* refers to oxytocin as the commitment neuromodulator because it reinforces the bonding process. In addition to orgasm, oxytocin is released when couples parent and nurture their children, and in women oxytocin is released during labour and breastfeeding.

Along with oxytocin, serotonin is also released following orgasm and works to regulate your mood, prompting feelings of cheerfulness, balance, and contentment. Serotonin works to relieve stress from the body, assisting with the immense feelings of relaxation that follow orgasm. The impact on the male's body often allows such an immense state of relaxation that he will fall asleep. This wonderful sense of euphoria provides such a replenishing rest for the body. Prolactin is a fascinating chemical that is also released following the peak of orgasm and relieves sexual arousal to take your mind off sex for a period of time. The purpose of this chemical is to allow the important rejuvenation of the body. As the prolactin gets released, so does a chemical called vasopressin, also known as the "pair-bonding chemical." This chemical is known for bonding the two intimate partners together, and it allows the body to support a monogamous relationship.

There are physical, emotional, and chemical elements at play that have a profound beneficial impact on the body during lovemaking and sex. It is interesting to note that many of the hormones and chemicals released during sex are the same ones used in many types of depression medications. While the external characteristics of the body draws you towards your partner, the internal chemicals are equally as fascinating, and their impact on the body must not be overlooked. Perhaps more sex is just what the doctor ordered.

Creating an Environment for Sex

In chapter 8 we explored the power of anchoring as stimuli that call forth certain states of mind. For example, when I hear a certain song, this stimulus takes me back to a time when Hayden and I first met. When the auditory stimulus (the song) is present, attached emotions of excitement, adventure, and new love are triggered as a result. With this in mind, it is important to create an environment in your bedroom that is conducive to seduction. The bedroom should serve just two purposes—sex and sleep. Create anchors that support these themes and notice the different energy that exists in your room once the environment is intentionally created.

As a quick recap, primary anchors can be visual (what we see), auditory (what we hear), and kinesthetic (what we feel). Beginning with visual anchors, have a think about the physical items, shapes, and symbols that are currently present in your bedroom. When Hayden and I first did this exercise, we were shocked at the amount of clutter and inappropriate items that were in our room. At the time we were living abroad in shared accommodation with limited space. Given the lack of private space, we had our photo board of all our friends and loved ones up on one wall of our bedroom. Yet when challenged by a mentor, we realised that the energy associated with our friends and family was the last thing we wanted in our room of intimacy. The photos were quickly removed and relocated to a savvy magnet system on the kitchen fridge, a more appropriate space of extended connection. We also had stacks of study books and resources on our bedside tables, items that should clearly be anchored with an office space. These were quickly removed, and we put a new rule in place that only books about fantasy and dream topics would stay by our bed, an approach we believe is conducive to the two core themes of sex and sleep. Once we got started, we went full steam ahead. The majority of the items in our room were cleared out, and we welcomed a clutter-free, cozy zone of intimacy. We introduced warm colours, lots of cushions, candles, symbolic art, and lamps for intimate lighting. The result was incredibly powerful. By simply changing the visual anchors in our bedroom, we created a space of increased intimacy purely anchored to sex, dreams, relevant conversation, and sleep.

**The bedroom should serve just two
purposes—sex and sleep.**

Next we talked about what we wanted to see more of in the bedroom in terms of bedroom attire. This part of the conversation gets wildly exciting, and it's fascinating to hear what turns the other person on the most in terms of visual elements and clothing (or lack of clothing). Find out from your lover what he or she finds the most visually appealing and what he or she would like to see more or less of. You may even discuss the different types of looks you give each other in the bedroom or the sexual positions that turn you on the most by the way each of you appear to the other. For many people a visually stimulating environment is essential when it comes to seduction in the bedroom.

Following our review of visual anchors, we considered the auditory anchors and made a small iPod dock available for background music. For some people music as part of the art of seduction is a must, while for others it is rather distracting. Talk about what type of music preferences are present in your own relationship. What music makes you feel sexy and incredibly turned on? Do you prefer sounds of nature, the waves of the ocean, wind swaying through the trees, or birds on a summer morning to create a seductive environment? Or perhaps you prefer silence? As part of this discussion on auditory anchors, a reflection on voice is also important. Talk to each other about the tone, pitch, and tempo of voice that turns you on the most. The point is that if you don't have the conversation, then you'll never know, so get talking!

As part of our review for creating anchors of passion and intimacy, we also thought about the kinesthetic anchors present in our room. We brought new, high-quality sheets and pillow sets. We talked about what we sleep in (or don't sleep in) in terms of comfort, and we discussed the feelings that we wanted to experience in our bedroom. We make a conscious effort to not argue or have disagreements in the bedroom, ensuring it remains a safe place anchored purely to sex and sleep. Some additional feelings to anchor in your bedroom may include being artful, fearless, adventurous, understanding, open, and vulnerable.

Once you've reviewed your bedroom and created the ideal anchors for intimacy and passion, it's then time to make sure the sexual activity is happening regularly based on the preferences within your relationship. Would you like to make love to your partner more or less often? What would be your ideal frequency?

If you are not currently having sex within your relationship, it is important that you work together to rebuild the attraction networks, to consciously reintroduce the fiery red spark back in to your love life. Providing a sense of being best friends is alive and strong in the relationship, where you would do anything for each other (as mentioned in chapter 3), then you can begin to rebuild the passion in the bedroom. If not, work on rebuilding the "best friends" element first and then move on to focusing on passion and sexual desire. In his book *The Brain that Changes Itself*, Norman Doidge describes how the brain is like a muscle that grows with exercise. He details the "use it or lose it" theory, which when applied to sexual passion and desire means the less often you have sex or create the emotions of hot, fiery passion in your relationship, the more disconnected you become with these concepts. On the other hand, the more you ensure passion and sexual desire exists, the more it will become embedded in your everyday experience of deep, lasting love and connection. It won't arrive packaged on your front doorstep, and instead if you want to experience fulfilling passion and desire, then you need to do it more often.

A Sexual Buffet

Couples with an incredibly active, healthy, and passionate sex life tend to have loads of variety both in life and in the bedroom. They have a varied range of options to choose from when it comes to making love and a strong understanding of what turns each person on. They also have the ability to communicate their needs and desires for sex effectively. They are able to talk about what feels good or what doesn't, what they'd like more of or less of, and how to meet their individual sexual needs and desires. They also have a range of ways to experience sex as part of their extensive sexual buffet.

**Variety is essential to an active,
healthy, and passionate sex life.**

Creating this degree of options when it comes to sex in your relationship is important. Just as most dessert menus have a selection of sweet-treat options, there are also different types of sex. The *Kama Sutra* is an ancient Indian Hindu text considered to be the primary work on human sexual behaviour in Sanskrit literature. In terms of creating your own sexual buffet of options, it's a great place to start. As an overarching summary, there are seven basic themes upon which the Hindu text is based. The *Kama Sutra* simply builds on these seven themes and adds a selection of variations for how each of the themes can take place. Firstly there is the male-on-top combination, which again can take place in many different styles, yet the positioning of the male energy on top is the basic theme. Next is the theme of female on top, once again with many different variations of this theme available. Thirdly the male enters from behind. Next is side by side from either behind or in front. Then there are the standing positions where the basic theme of this category is the upright positioning, which again can take on a variety of forms. The sixth category is kneeling, and the seventh category is sitting. All of these seven themes encompass a variety of positions and allow different sensations during intercourse. Add a touch of wildly crazy, steady, raunchy, or soft and slow, and you have an increased sexual buffet to create the ultimate selection of choice when it comes to sizzle between the sheets.

To complement the range of positions, language, tonality, and physiology are also important. What words turn you on, and in what tone of voice? Language and the words we use in the bedroom can be defined through three categories—clinical, neutral, and slang words. Clinical words are the medical terms like vagina, penis, clitoris, etc. They are not particularly sexy. Next is the neutral language that is often the bridge between the clinical terms and the more extreme slang. Neutral language includes words and phrases like "love button," "big boy," and "hot spot," often labeled by the couple, creating a sense of familiarity and comfort in the sex language space. This category includes the times when couples create nicknames for certain parts of the body. Thirdly slang language refers to the more extreme references to body parts, such as cock, pussy, and fucking as opposed to making love. Slang language often differs depending on age groups. It's important to have a range of language available to increase the variety in your sex life. Talk with your lover about what language category you prefer and explore ways to venture across all three.

In addition, the delivery of the words adds energy and works to give them added meaning. There are different ways sex talk can be conveyed with varying tone of voice and physiology. For example, delivery can range from soft and sensual with a gentle physiology to loud and abrupt with a strong, confident approach. Have a play with a variety of options and then discuss which approaches you prefer best.

Following the exploration of language and selection of positions, three different types of sex exist to build variety. The quickie is the quick-release type of sex that tends to last for no more than two or three minutes. The main purpose is the release of tension and a quick bit of fun on the side. It's really important that this type of sex is allowed in a relationship, and that sex doesn't always need to involve a long lovemaking session. Quick and to the point, this type of sex can be done almost anywhere and can encourage creativity on location.

Next is maintenance sex. This type of sex usually lasts for anywhere between fifteen to thirty minutes and is just as the name suggests, *maintenance* to meet the sexual needs of both partners. The frequency of maintenance sex varies in different relationships, and the conversation needs to take place in terms of how often each lover would prefer to have sex and what type. The idea is that you and your lover create the options available on the sexual buffet, which you can then choose from as you please. Couples with a strong passionate element tend to be good at regular doses of both the quickie and maintenance sexual sessions, yet the final type of sex is the one that gets left off the list in far too many relationships. It's the gourmet sex.

As the name suggests, gourmet sex is elaborately prepared, fancy, and specialised. It might involve getting a hotel room for the weekend and leaving in the set of clothes you arrive in or going to bed early for an hours-on-end gourmet session or sleeping in on the weekend with no plans on the agenda except each other. The point is not necessarily to be having sex the whole weekend, evening or morning, but instead to create the space for intimacy and further exploration. You might light candles, play music, enjoy fine wine and food, order room service, take long baths or hot showers together, explore massage, or play with a range of sex toys. It's about saying yes to each other and taking the time out to make the passion in your relationship your whole focus.

What types of sex currently exist in your relationship, and when was the last time you took the time out for some true gourmet sex? When I ask this question to couples, often I hear the responses, "We don't have the time," "We can't afford a hotel," or, "Who will look after the kids?" My responses are always along the same lines. At what point did you choose to settle for mediocrity when it comes to passion in your love life? What part of you doesn't believe you are worthy of taking the time out to build a phenomenal connection with your lover? Is your relationship worth investing in? If the outcome you want to achieve is a happy, fulfilling relationship, then you must commit to directing energy in that direction. Given you've made it to chapter 9 of this book, my guess is that you've absolutely got what it takes to reach your relationship goals. You've got the drive and commitment, and now you've got added tools and practical strategies to assist you on your way.

Understanding and celebrating the differences between men and woman is important when it comes to relationship success. In terms of sexual passion, as a general rule men are predominantly more physical creatures. They are hunters and typically associate availability with proximity. This means the physical availability of a man's partner for him points to emotional and sexual availability, and because this is in some ways assumed, it is something he may not necessarily feel the need to communicate, sometimes to his detriment. Women, on the other hand, are reflective creatures. As part of their nature, they tend to think about the bigger picture, not just the part that they can see or touch. For women, physicality grows out of emotions. It is therefore emotional availability that activates the female physical and sexual natures. Woman will stop sex whenever they are not feeling safe or comfortable and will also hold out on making love if their needs outside of the relationship are not being taken care of. Women are more ready to show up physically and sexually when their partner is emotionally present, while men tend to simply show up with their emotional presence often something of an afterthought.

When it comes to approaching sex, these types of differences help in understanding the motives of males and females. When you understand the male connection with proximity equals intimacy compared to the female connection of emotions and intimacy, you can then work to better understand each other. These core themes coupled with the sexual buffet of variety equip you with the ideal toolkit for increased intimacy and passion in your love life.

Given all that you now know, choose to break the cycle of declination and instead adopt a cycle of intensification, where the sexual passion within your relationship increases with time. I promise you'll be the hit topic at your next coffee catch-up when everyone goes to complain about the lack of sex in their relationship—insert excuse here—and instead you kick off with a satisfying statement about the sizzle between your sheets.

Chapter Summary

From exploring the passionate drive of opposing masculine and feminine energies to delving into sexual archetypes, discussing the power of the body, and detailing ideas for a sexual buffet of variety, I trust this chapter has inspired you to spice it up in the bedroom. This chapter as the cherry on top is particularly important because there is an entire world of discovery that exists within the passionate element of love. When it comes to sex and the power of the body, you must adopt a youthful sense of curiosity and be open and willing to make changes in the areas where you want new or improved results. Go forth and explore. You can thank me later.

Exercises for Reflection

Increasing Your Sexual Buffet

Choose a favourite dessert that both you and your lover enjoy. Book a date night, light the candles, and sit down to discuss the fiery spark of passionate desire in your relationship.

Using the information shared in this chapter, create conversations about attraction, lovemaking, and sex. Use the following questionnaire to share your individual thoughts and insights and then commit to increasing your sexual buffet and investing even more energy into this incredibly important part of your relationship.

1. If you were to assess the sexual polarity (the power arching between masculine and feminine poles) that exists in your current love life, what would it be? For example, Hamish and Sarah selected 80 per cent to 20 per cent, where Hamish was very strongly taking on the masculine role in the bedroom.

2. Do your results support creating the sexual passion that exists when opposites attract? If not, what are the next steps you are going to take to move towards your desired outcome?

3. What would you like to see more of or less of in the bedroom?

4. Would you like to make love more or less often? What would be your ideal frequency?

5. What sexual archetypes turn you on the most?

Three strong female archetypes include the following:
• Courtesan
• Seductress
• Dominatrix

Three key male archetypes include the following:
• Toy Boy
• Seducer (or Sensualist)
• Alpha

6. What sexual archetypes do you and your loved one currently resemble the most?

7. What sexual archetypes are you most looking forward to exploring further?

8. What's your favourite body part, and why?

9. What is it about the way your loved one dresses and acts that really gets you going?

10. What do your clothes say about you? As a female, do you embrace feminine, flowing materials, colours, patterns,

and dresses, or does your wardrobe represent more sharp-edged pants, suits, and collars? As a male, do you dress like a man or a boy? Are your shirts pressed and mature or covered in childlike art and imagery?

11. Is your bedroom currently conducive to an intimate zone that supports the two primary purposes of sex and sleep? What *visual* elements need to be removed/introduced? What *auditory* elements need to be removed/introduced? What *kinesthetic* elements need to be removed/introduced?

12. Reflect on the following list of sex options and circle the words that best reflect the current themes in your relationship. Next place a star by the themes you would like to see more of. Consider doing this part of the questionnaire separately and then comparing answers at the end.

Sex positions
Him on top
Her on top
Him entering from behind
Side by side (front and back)
Standing

Kneeling

Sitting

Language

Clinical

Neutral

Slang

Tone of voice

Silence

Soft

Sensual

Loud

Abrupt

Confident

Types of sex

Quickie

Maintenance

Gourmet

Following the completion of the twelve questions and enjoyment of your dessert, detail below the five key insights you and your loved one have committed to introducing to your own sexual buffet.

Commitment: It is one week from now (insert date) and we have successfully introduced the following five key elements to our own sexual buffet of variety:

1 _____

2 _____

3 _____

4 _____

5 _____

The one-week time frame is designed to fuel action. The brain loves commitment and completion, so make a statement and then make it happen.

Closing Gifts of Gratitude

Creating Relationship Success in the Heart of Your Home

What philosophy of love are you going
to pass on to generations to come?

If you are ever asked if you've heard the theory of the jelly bean jar, you can now squash it out by upping the ante and sharing the theory of *Love on the Kitchen Table*. Tell your lucky listeners that they have to build a strong foundation for the table because the love action will be long-lasting, intense, and completely fulfilling. Watch and cherish their reaction as they become totally bewildered by the gift of someone speaking positively about the power of love. The skeptics are the ones who are looking for the most answers. Back yourself and gift them with your newfound knowledge to shake their maps of the world. Scream from the rooftops a better way to *do* love. Love is a verb. To experience it more often, you must do it more often. You must invest in creating your ideal relationship and then commit to living it. When you know more, you can do more, and when you are clear on your own beliefs, values, and desired outcomes for success in love, then you can manifest exactly what you ask for.

People are naturally attracted to others who know what they want and are drawn to those who back themselves. Watch as your ripple effect begins to impact the world around you. When you become the change you wish to see, amazing things begin to happen. We all go through life with the gift of great teachers, models, and mentors. Despite their significant influence, who you become is ultimately the result of how you apply what you have been taught. As an individual on a constant journey of growth, you must transmute the information you learn into a living philosophy, and the same is true within your relationship. What philosophy of love are you going to pass on to the generations to come?

One of the most important things you can do to improve the success in your relationship is to get educated about the differences between men and woman and to seek information about human behaviour models and patterns of behaviour that impact your everyday lives. Fortunately there has been an extraordinarily amount of data gathered regarding gender differences in the last decade, and this information is now easily and readily available. If this is one of many relationship books you have read, then I trust it has served you well and added to the abundance of valuable knowledge and insights that exist in our literary world today. If this is a first for you, then my ultimate desire is that it has fueled your interest in wanting to know more. Whether a particular topic has caught your eye or the insights have simply sparked your desire to learn more, I applaud you for your commitment to personal growth, and I'm eternally grateful for the changes you are already making through the ripple effect of your thoughts.

Your presence as part of this book says a lot about who you are. You are already committed to evolving beyond the patterns of your past to break through to a life that is centred on an expression of the deeper potentials you hold for love, connection, and your relationships. You are the first example of how you expect the world to treat you. Knowing all that you now know, may you go forth and buck the trends of society to create a relationship where passion thrives.

From my heart to yours, I wish you well.

Influences

Adler, Harry, and Heather Beryl. 1999. *NLP in 21 Days.* London: Piatkus Books, Brown Book Group

Carnarius, Rosemarie. 2012. *Liberating Masculine and Feminine: Breaking the Spell of Excursion.* West Conshohocken, PA: Infinity Publishing

Chapman, Gary D. 1992. *The 5 Love Languages.* Chicago: Northfield Publishing

Chapman, Gary D. 2005. *The Four Seasons of Marriage.* Tyndale House Publishers, Inc.

Copprue, Tanya. 2010. *The Secret of Masculine and Feminine Energies: A Guide to Healing Relationships.* Soul De Diva Press

Deida, David. 2004. *The Way of the Superior Man.* Colorado: Sounds True, Boulder

Demartini, John. 2008. *The Gratitude Effect*. Australia: New Holland Publishers

Demartini, John. 2010. *Inspired Destiny: Living a Fulfilling and Purposeful Life*. Hay House, Inc.

Doidge, Norman, MD. 2007. *The Brain That Changes Itself*. Penguin Books, Ltd.

Glover, Robert. 2000. *No More Mr. Nice Guy*. Philadelphia, PA: Running Press Book Publishers

Gottman, John, PhD. 1999. *The Seven Principles for Making Marriage Work*. New York: Three Rivers Press

Gray, John. 1993. *Men Are from Mars, Women Are from Venus*. HarperCollins e-books

Hill, Napoleon. 1937. *Think and Grow Rich*. The Ralston Society

Miller, George A., Eugene Galanter, and Karl H. Pibram. 1960. *Plans and the Structure of Behaviour*. New York: Henry Holt & Company

Myss, Caroline. 2013. *Archetypes*. Australia: Hay House

Nemeth, Maria. 1997. *The Energy of Money*. New York: The Ballantine Publishing Group

Pease, Allan and Barbara. 2004. *The Definitive Book of Body Language*. New York: Bantam Dell, a division of Random House, Inc.

Peck, Scott. 1978. *The Road Less Traveled*. New York: Touchstone, Rockefeller Centre

Redford, James. 1993. *The Celestine Prophecy*. New York: Warner Books, Inc.

Robbins, Anthony. 1992. *Awaken the Giant Within*. London: Pocket Books, Simon & Schuster

Venker, Suzanne and Phyllis Schlafly. 2010. *The Flipside of Feminism*. Washington, DC: WorldNetDaily